74276.

YOGA

YOGA

BY

HARI PRASAD SHASTRI

W. & G. FOYLE LTD.
119-125, CHARING CROSS ROAD, LONDON, W.C.2.

First published 1957
Reprinted June, 1958
Reprinted 1966
© W. & G. Foyle Ltd.

Printed in Great Britain by
Love & Malcomson Ltd., Brighton Road, Redhill, Surrey

CONTENTS

FOREWORD

Hari Prasad Shastri was born at Bareilly in Northern India in 1881. He came from a long line of Brahmin scholars and himself took the highest possible distinctions in Sanskrit and in the classical philosophy of India. He was also well versed in the Chinese, Japanese and Persian languages and literatures. He studied the practical methods of Yoga as a traditional disciple under the saint Shri Dada of Aligarh. At the age of 20 he undertook an arduous pilgrimage to Tibet and was permitted by the late Tashi Lama to bring back many valuable manuscripts to India. In 1916 he went to Japan, where he lectured on Hindu philosophy at Waseda University and the Imperial University in Tokyo. Later he became dean of Hardoon University in Shanghai and Professor of Philosophy at Nankwang College. Dr. Sun Yat Sen, founder and first President of the Republic of China, was Dr. Shastri's personal friend and pupil. While in China he founded the *Asiatic Review* and brought out the standard Chinese edition of the Buddhist Scriptures now used in the Universities. He also translated the *Analects* of Confucius into Hindi, and supervised a translation of the *Koran* into Chinese.

Dr. Shastri came to London in 1929, where he founded Shanti Sadan, a traditional centre of the classical Yoga of Self-realisation. Before his death in 1956, Dr. Shastri gave detailed instructions for the continuance of his work, and his pupils are carrying on his yogic centre according to his directions at Shanti Sadan, 29 Chepstow Villas, London, W.11. Among Dr. Shastri's literary works, his translation of the Indian epic *Ramayana* was sponsored by the Indian Government. The present book was begun by Dr. Shastri before his death and has been completed from his notes.

INTRODUCTION

YOGA is the spiritual science of being and becoming; it is not for the unpractical or the dreamy. The Teachers of old had illumined minds, but acute and critical ones also, and they held nothing too sacred for investigation and discussion. Indeed this attitude has survived to the present day, for the would-be pupil is expected to enquire and experiment before he is allowed to practise Yoga seriously. There are of course spurious and debased forms of Yoga, but the traditional Yoga which is dealt with in this handbook is not something which fears reason. It does not depend on psychic or occult phenomena and may be practised safely by any sincere student.

All wish to live free, free from the tyranny of the mind and the senses, and also from the fear of adverse circumstances. Restriction is always painful, and man will never be satisfied while he is subject to it. His search after pleasure, power, wealth and knowledge is the outer sign of his need and instinctive longing for expansion and freedom. After making countless experiments which lead nowhere, at last he turns his attention in on himself, and seeks truth there and not in outer experience. Then Yoga, having revealed the goal and the significance of his search to him, proceeds to give the method whereby it may be realized. This method cannot be practised successfully where there is prejudice or enmity towards others, or where it is employed to run away from life and its responsibilities. The chief aim of the Yoga is to give the aspirant first an intellectual idea and then a direct vision of Truth and his identity with it. Through this progressive awareness of his true nature, the Yoga teaches him how to live as a master of circumstance and at home in any walk of life.

Most men live instinctively and are therefore at the mercy of their minds, their instincts and their circumstances. This involves waste of energy and time, and the Teachers of Yoga have always placed great importance on the production and conservation of power, both spiritual and mental. According to them, real life begins only when an attempt has been made to control the mind. Although, in the last analysis, Yoga is the science of spirit which is beyond the mind, at the outset it is mainly concerned with mental training. The first objective therefore is to bring the mind into focus, and then to place it under observation by the aid of ancient and tested methods, some of which are given in this handbook. Practices leading to the directing and stopping of the mind are also given, for only when these can be performed with some degree of success can any control be said to be present. No one would claim to be able to drive a car who could only start it and then accelerate. He must also be able to steer and stop it at will, if he is not to be a menace on the public highway. The preliminary exercises leading to mastery of the mind are traditional, and have been tested by thousands of aspirants over the centuries.

Some may ask why it is necessary to have recourse to a science at all, in order to live well. The answer is that just as we can only command Nature through observing her laws, and not through the exercise of arbitrary force, so in the psychological realm also, recognition of and obedience to the spiritual law of Unity which governs the Universe brings harmony and freedom.

There are mighty powers hidden behind the mind, but they will not come into focus or operation until the mind has been controlled, stilled and then directed towards the Self within. The bough of a tree or even a straw close to the eyes can hide the sun from the gaze, and it will not become visible until the obstruction has been removed. Meditation leads to the removal of the barrier put up by the undisciplined mind, and allows the supra-mental consciousness to function. When this takes place, the aspirant realises that he is already divine in essence, that there is in fact no impassable gulf fixed between himself and the supreme Reality, and that it is in his power to make his place of living as wide as space or as restricted as the point of a needle.

There is a verse in the Bhagavad Gita which says: "In this path no effort is ever lost; even a little practice of this discipline protects one from great fear", and it is claimed by the Yoga that, provided he carries out the instructions in a responsible manner, the student will from the outset receive great psychological benefits which will enable him to stabilize his faculties and his life. The inner significance of the science of Yoga, however, will only reveal itself slowly to him as he goes deeper and deeper into it, and the final revelation of Truth will come as the result of spiritual maturity, and will take place through direct inner experience and not through mental channels.

1

THE HISTORY AND LITERATURE OF YOGA

TRADITIONALLY Yoga is the divine science, a gift of God to His creation. When man has reached a certain stage of evolution, the Yoga is "revealed" to a few sages who are empowered to transmit it to qualified pupils and through them to successive generations. The earliest archaeological evidence for the practice of Yoga is afforded by some small figures of men in the posture of yogic meditation excavated in the Indus valley. They date from at least 3000 B.C. The earliest literary evidence is to be found in references to the practice of Yoga in the Vedas, the oldest books in the world, parts of which are held by scholars to have been composed in Northern India not later than 2500 B.C.; and the tradition is that the Yoga existed and was handed down orally for thousands of years before that.

THE UPANISHADS

Later in time than the hymns of the Vedas came a number of treatises called Upanishads, in which the expert practicants of Yoga summarized their high mystical experiences. The Upanishads supply the doctrinal foundation of all yogic teaching and rank among the most wonderful productions of the human mind. They are neither pure philosophy nor pure theology in the Western sense. In the form in which they have come down to us, many of them are compilations and their contents range from metaphysics and ethical instruction to practical guidance on the observance of ritual sacrifices. The central message of the Upanishads is that the consciousness which underlies the personality of man is not really limited by that personality but is in fact the support of the entire universe. Through a life of self-discipline and tireless benevolence and through the sustained practice of meditation a man can become aware of the infinite, timeless and changeless consciousness that illumines his intellect and supports the universe of changing forms and appearances. All other goals that man proposes to himself are ultimately delusive in the sense that they will never give him lasting satisfaction.

THE EPICS AND THE BHAGAVAD GITA

After the Upanishads but before the birth of the Buddha in the sixth century B.C. there appeared, again in Northern India, two vast epic poems known as the *Ramayana* and the *Mahabharata*. The *Ramayana*, which is couched in poetic language of the highest order, contains little instruction in meditation or the technical practices of Yoga, but the lives of its main characters are models of ideal human behaviour in an active life in the world. The hero, Ramachandra, is held by Hindus to have been an Incarnation of God on earth. A continuation of the *Ramayana* entitled the *Yoga Vasishtha*, which was written later, supplies direct teaching about yogic practice which supplements the ethical teaching of the *Ramayana*.

The *Mahabharata* is an encyclopaedic work of immense length and contains many important passages of direct yogic teaching interspersed amid the epic narrative of military struggles. The most famous and important of these is the *Bhagavad Gita*, a poem of 700 couplets in which God, incarnated as the charioteer Krishna, instructs the warrior Arjuna in the general moral and spiritual principles which should govern the life of the yogi, especially the yogi who practises Yoga while actively fulfilling his duties in the world. If the *Bhagavad Gita* is read with Shankaracharya's classical commentary, it furnishes the best available all-round guide to the theory and practice of Yoga.

PATANJALI

Later in point of time than the *Bhagavad Gita* come the *Yoga Sutras* of Patanjali, with the classical commentary of Vyasa. Patanjali gives detailed references to points of technique in the practice of meditation which are of interest to the student who has already advanced to a certain degree, but the philosophical framework in which his teaching is set differs in certain respects from the Advaita (non-dualism) of Shankaracharya. Moreover, his work is of interest only in its exposition of particular details of technique, since the discipline he describes cannot be carried out in its entirety in the course of active life under conditions in a modern Western society. Patanjali's statement of the moral prerequisites for the life of Yoga (truthfulness, non-stealing, continence, friendliness, compassion, etc.), is valuable for all students.

SHANKARACHARYA

With Shankaracharya we come to the greatest single figure in the history of Yoga. Like many a great yogi of the present and the past, he hid his individual personality behind his work, and not even the date at which he lived is known to us. His major writings were his commentaries on twelve individual Upanishads, on the *Bhagavad Gita* and on an important work summarising the Upanishads called the *Vedanta Sutras*. He also wrote independent philosophical works in verse and prose of great mystical insight and literary charm. The writings of Shankaracharya were first brought to the notice of the Western world at the end of the last century by the German scholar Paul Deussen. Although Deussen did not penetrate to the real inner significance of Shankaracharya's writings, even so he pronounced them, in sheer intellectual ability, equal in rank with the writings of Plato and Kant.

One of Shankaracharya's conspicuous merits was his ability to handle difficult metaphysical questions with relative ease and simplicity. Another was his breadth of vision, which enabled him to exhibit the latent unity of doctrine amid the apparent diversity of the texts on which he commented. Above all, his personal success on the practical path of Yoga enabled him to discuss the passages of the Upanishads and *Bhagavad Gita* which deal with practical mysticism with the ease and familiarity of a person to whom all levels of the subject under discussion were known through personal experience. Nearly everything Shankaracharya wrote is available in English translation. His longer independent mystical poems such as the "Crest Jewel of Wisdom" (*Vivekachudamani*), the "Direct Experience of Reality" (*Aparokshanubhuti*), the "Knowledge of the Self"

(*Atmabodha*) and the "Explanation of the Text" (*Vakyavritti*), form admirable "vade-mecums" for the student of Yoga. A reliable translation of his commentary on the *Bhagavad Gita* has been published by A. Mahadev Sastri in Madras.

AFTER SHANKARACHARYA

Shankaracharya's own writings were comparatively simple, but his doctrines were worked out in great detail by a long series of brilliant thinkers culminating in Madhusudana Sarasvati of Benares in the sixteenth century A.D. Among the most famous names are Padmapada and Sureshvara (both personal pupils of Shankaracharya) and Vidyaranya Swami, a genius who founded a political empire in the first part of his life and later wrote two philosophical classics after taking the orange robe of a monk. These writers are highly technical, and no adequate history of the great metaphysical movement they represent has yet been written in any European language. All of them wrote in Sanskrit, the sacred language of India, a rich and flexible medium, admirable alike for conveying noble sentiments and subtle intellectual speculation. But during the Indian Middle Ages the practice began to spread of writing simple devotional literature in the spoken languages of the people. Especially worthy of mention are the devotional works in Hindi of Kabir, Surdas and Tulsidas in the fifteenth and sixteenth centuries. Kabir was unorthodox doctrinally, but his poems, some of which have been translated into English by the modern poet Rabindranath Tagore, throw light on the mystical aspects of the yogic path. Surdas dwelt on the love of the cowherd maidens of Braj for the youthful Krishna as a symbol of the union of the soul with God in mystical ecstasy. Tulsidas conveyed many inner secrets of the life of Yoga in the course of retelling the epic tale of the Ramayana in the Hindi vernacular. The tradition of teaching Yoga through the medium of devotional poetry has continued into modern times. Among the great yogis of Northern India who were teaching by this method at the close of the last century were Swami Nirbhayananda and Swami Rama Tirtha.

YOGA IS UNIVERSAL

The practice of Yoga originated in India, and the metaphysical view of the world which is revealed to the yogi in the highest stages of the path was first formulated in the Upanishads and later worked out in detail by Shankaracharya and the writers of his school. For practical purposes, no doubt, it is best to study the doctrine and the method as laid down in the Indian classics. But the yogis of India do not claim a monopoly of spiritual wisdom. For instance, they revere Christ and Buddha as Incarnations of God, and Mohammed as a great and holy prophet, and they hold that mystics of all genuine faiths have attained a direct insight into the nature of reality. For the yogis, Truth alone is the highest object of reverence, and they judge the teachings of other prophets and philosophers in the light of their own personal experience of this Truth. In a sense, therefore, "the literature of Yoga" may be said to include all that has been written anywhere at a high level of inspiration touching the nature of man and of the world and of ultimate reality. The doctrines and practices of Yoga, coloured by Buddhist ideas, were carried to China and thence to Japan by Buddhist missionaries. They quickened the indigenous cultures of these countries and raised the tone of the mental atmosphere. Sublime masterpieces of painting, sculpture and poetry were left as a permanent record of their effectiveness in heightening the spiritual awareness of man. It is no less possible that Yoga may bring about a world-wide spiritual renaissance to-day if it is practised by sufficient people in its classical and traditional form. Perhaps signs of it are already beginning to appear.

2

THE PHILOSOPHY OF YOGA

THE Sanskrit word for philosophy is 'darshana' which literally means 'sight'. It means the search after the ultimate truth of life in the world. Consciously, or more usually unconsciously, everyone is trying to discover the reality behind the experiences of their daily lives. Intellectually this search expresses itself as the hunger for knowledge. It is not only feminine curiosity which remains unsated: the scientist unceasingly probing the 'how' by experiment and the child persistently asking 'why?' are manifesting a characteristic which is deeply engrained in every human personality. Emotionally, the same urge can be recognized in the universal desire to be happy and to avoid sorrow and suffering.

THE FUNCTION OF PHILOSOPHY

In the West, the philosopher's approach to truth takes the form of an intellectual effort for completely unified knowledge. Philosophy is not looked upon as an important phase of life. A handful of learned University Professors can enjoy it as an intellectual pastime while other members of society dispense with it and concentrate on 'doing things'. But, according to Yoga, philosophy is of prime importance and all other branches of knowledge and departments of life should look to it for inspiration. Its main field is *an enquiry into the nature of man himself* and the discovery of a principle of unity and immutability, free from discord and contradiction, which is recognised as Absolute. Here all 'how' and 'why' is silenced for ever. Here man feels that all his faculties have finally come to fruition. 'On attaining which, nothing in the world still remains to be attained' is the description given in the Upanishad. This touch with the Absolute, this vision of Self, makes him feel perfect. It is a direct and lasting experience of Reality, which defies description in words.

THE VEDANTA

The word 'Yoga', which means 'yoke' or 'union' (i.e. union of the individual soul with God), is commonly used in its more restricted meaning of 'the practice of mind control'. It is defined by Patanjali as 'the restraint of the modes of the mind' and in the Bhagavad Gita as 'mental balance' (samatva). A good general description of Yoga given in Chapter VI of the Bhagavad Gita is reproduced on page 82. The intellectual basis of Yoga is furnished by the Vedanta, a system of thought which draws its inspiration from the metaphysical reflections of the great Seers (Rishis) of the Upanishads such as Yajnavalkya, Uddalaka and Angiras. In Vedanta the deep intuitive experience of these Rishis is the vital and fundamental fact; the variations in the exposition of the philosophy by later writers are seen as but intellectual glosses on this fact, which is essentially beyond proof or disproof by the human reason, although it can be confirmed in experience if the requisite discipline is followed.

The practical nature of Yoga insists that the intellectual no less than the emotional resources of man should be harnessed to lead the yogi to the same experience of which the Rishis speak. One of the earliest classical commentators on the Brihadaranyaka Upanishad wrote: "By whatever statement a knowledge of the inner Self can be imparted to man, that is the right one: there is no one dogma fixed for all". Philosophical reflection (vichara) ceases to be an end in itself as a system of metaphysical enquiry and becomes, in the guise of inward self-analysis, a potent means of mind-training.

REASON AND INTUITION

The function of reason is to make explicit the spiritual experience revealed by the Seers, not only for the sake of the individual himself but also for the benefit of those with whom he comes into contact. In this context emphasis is laid upon the limitations and secondary place of reason—a difference from the exaggerated respect often accorded to it in our own 20th century. Revelation (Shruti) and the help of a competent teacher versed in the tradition are of much greater importance to the yogi than the possession of a brilliant intellect. Purely intellectual knowledge moves round its object and studies it from a distance, like food held in the palm of the hand, whereas intuitive understanding, when rightly guided, embraces and absorbs what is to be known, like food which is digested and absorbed into the body. Such intuitive understanding is direct, immediate and unrelational, and only through it can we know the object as it really is. Reason can take us only so far, like a rocket which assists the take-off of a high-flying plane; at a certain point reason is discarded and drops away, its task accomplished, and the soul soars upward alone into the region of pure knowledge.

THE TEACHER (GURU).

The key to the successful application of this technique is the gift of a spiritual teacher (Guru). "That knowledge is not to be obtained by reasoning", says the Katha Upanishad, "but when it is taught to you by another (i.e. by a competent teacher), O dearest, it is easy to understand". A Guru must be "versed in the Scriptures and centred in God" (Mundaka Upanishad). This does not mean that he has to be a scholar; it implies that he knows the inner meaning of the texts and is competent to pass it on to others out of his compassion. A Guru does not pretend to be an innovator; his teaching is prefaced, like every Buddhist Sutra, not with 'this is what *I* teach' but with 'thus I have heard'. He must have a mandate to teach and have had the tradition passed down to him by word of mouth from his own teacher. Many Saints of God have not been teachers.

Not all teachers follow the same mode of life: some are monks, some are laymen, some are statesmen and some live in semi-obscurity. It is stated in the Upanishads that only a person who has fulfilled certain conditions which entitle him to the teaching is attracted to a teacher. The would-be pupil must have been convinced that the objects of the world cannot give him lasting satisfaction, and he must to some extent have eradicated from his heart the faults of pride, egoity, self-superiority and love of power, and have achieved control over his senses.

In Yoga, as in a craft, the apprentice can gain a certain theoretical acquaintance with the subject through studying books and applying his mind to it, but he is unlikely to become a master craftsman unless he has studied under a master craftsman. The secrets of Yoga can only be transmitted to receptive and carefully-trained minds with each of which the teacher has established an unique relationship.

SUMMARY OF ADVAITA (NON-DUALISM)

. There are six main systems in Indian philosophy of which the Advaita Vedanta is the last and the most complete. To a great extent the six systems may be said to be complementary to one another, and the Advaita borrows extensively from the other five. What follows is a necessarily brief summary of Advaita Vedanta, based on the writings of the acknowledged master-philosopher of Yoga, Shri Shankaracharya.

The essence of the philosophy of Advaita is to be found in the couplet:

> *Brahman sattyam jagan mithya*
> *Jivo Brahmaiva na parah.*
> God is real, the world is illusory,
> The individual soul and God are one and the same.

There is a mystery hidden in the commonest objects of the world. 'Ordinariness' is the veil hiding the extraordinary. It is our common experience that 'things are not what they seem'. For instance, a writer is sitting at what seems to him a solid writing desk, brown in colour and smooth to the touch. But is it really 'solid', 'brown' and 'smooth'? A more searching analysis shows this picture painted by his senses to be an illusion. The desk is not 'solid' but a large number of disconnected particles gyrating in space; as the light changes, the particular 'brown' colour also changes; and the 'smooth' surface is shown up under a microscope as a fiercely jagged edge.

The notions of time, space and causation which are the framework of the world experience can also be shown to be self-contradictory and logically inexplicable. For instance, the writer says that 'the desk changes' from moment to moment because of the different configuration of atoms or the alteration in the light. This involves the contradiction that something which remains the same, namely 'the desk', becomes different. In this respect the Vedanta anticipates the conclusion of the English philosopher F. H. Bradley, that "the world, as so understood, contradicts itself and is therefore appearance and not Reality".

GOD AND THE WORLD

The created universe is called in Vedanta 'the ever-moving' (jagat) because its nature is a continual state of flux, or 'the ocean of becoming' (sansara) because it is unfathomable as an ocean and never static for a moment. Shri Shankara reasons that that which is changing implies something that is changeless. Change signifies flow or movement against an unchanging background—otherwise no change would ever be recognizable. Even an illusion or a sheer imagination must stand upon some ground. From the practical point of view, all of us desire the security of the changeless but seek it wrongly in the changing world of forms which consistently dashes our hopes. Shri Shankara concludes that we can attain security, peace and happiness by coming to recognize the reality of the changeless ground and the illusory nature of the changing phenomena.

Of what nature is this world-illusion and how is it related to the ground upon which it rests? In theological terms, what is the relation between the world and God?

To illustrate his reply to this question, Shri Shankara uses a classical simile of Vedanta. A peasant returning one evening from the fields thinks he sees a snake coiled up in the corner of his hut. He is greatly alarmed until he goes nearer with a lamp to investigate and finds the 'snake' to be a harmless rope. Here the rope stands for the Reality (Brahman) which is the unchanging ever-present canvas of Existence, Consciousness and Infinity upon which the transient pictures of the world are forever being painted and passing away. The snake is the world superimposed as phenomenal 'names and forms' on the underlying Reality. The peasant imagines that he sees every detail of the snake from its menacing hood to its tail, and each of these details has a distinct 'form' to which he gives the 'name 'of 'hood', 'tail', 'scales', 'forked tongue' and so forth. His mind becomes agitated and he is afraid that the snake will strike and,

if not kill him, at least cause him the agony of severe poisoning.
This fear, agitation and suffering is due only to his ignorance
of the true nature of the snake, which is that of a harmless and
useful rope. By the light of the lamp he discovers this, and all
his anxieties are at an end. In the same way the light of spiritual
knowledge gives a realization of the nature of God (Brahman)
and the unreality of worldly values, and thereafter all sorrow
and suffering is at an end.

GOD (BRAHMAN) AND THE INDIVIDUAL SOUL (JIVA)

Brahman not only underlies the 'names and forms' which are
identifiable as the objects seen in the external world. Our bodies
and minds also form part of that world, and Brahman is to be
found buried deep beneath the superimpositions of our personalities. This is the significance of the second half of the couplet
already quoted:
"The individual soul and God are one and the same".
The purpose of the methods of Yoga is to enable man to realize
this identity, which for most people is obscured.

The unchanging ever-present canvas of Existence, Consciousness and Infinity is at the root of our personalities, and indeed
everyone is in some measure aware of the fact. No-one doubts
his own existence or his nature as consciousness. Shri Shankara
advances this as one of the strongest logical confirmations of the
identity of the Self and Brahman. There can only be one
Existence and one Consciousness, which is infinite and all-
pervasive, he reasons. It is by discovering God (Brahman)
within the personality that a man fulfils the purpose of life.
In the Bhagavad Gita (IV. 42), Shri Krishna exhorts Prince
Arjuna:
"Therefore, with the sword of wisdom cleave asunder all
doubts born of ignorance about the Self hidden in the
intellect, and resort to Yoga".

THE NATURE OF THE SELF

The old Delphic motto 'Know Thyself' implies that man
does not know his own nature completely and in truth. The
Yoga accepts the same premise. Just as the illusory snake is

superimposed on the rope, so an illusory personality is super-imposed on the real Self (Atman or Brahman). Thus a man tends to think of himself as other than he is; his real Universal Self is obscured by the cocoon of false identification with the body, mind and senses which is spun over it, and he imagines himself to be a limited individual soul (jiva). For instance, he thinks: "I am an Englishman, 30 years old, tall and rather sunburnt", whereas these are all attributes of the body. He may regard himself as possessing a good ear for music or as being rather short-sighted, which are really comments on the sensory apparatus. He may feel that he is clever and energetic, and is probably conscious of having a limited individuality different from other people and of being sometimes happy and at other times depressed; these are all in fact modes of mind and ego. The changeless element within the personality, which provides the background against which all the changes in body and mind from infancy onwards take place, is essentially unconnected with those changes. It is their witness (sakshi) in the same sense as a lamp hanging from the centre of a room 'witnesses' and illumines whatever goes on in the room when occupied and the absence of all activity when the room is empty. The activities of the body and mind in the waking state and of the mind in dream, as well as the absence of mental activity in dreamless sleep, all take place in the light of the Self.

THE SELF IS NOT THE MIND OR BODY

The changeless can never be identical with the changing; the Witness can never be the same as what is witnessed. The Self is therefore essentially different from the body and the mind. Shri Shankara advances these arguments in the following verses of *The Explanation of the Text* (Vakyavritti):

"The seer of a pot is ever different from the pot, its object, and is never one with the pot. Similarly, the seer of the body is ever different from the body, its object. Therefore the truth is: 'I am not the body'. This you must understand.

The same reasoning shows that I, who am the witness of the senses, am not the senses. Thus I am not the mind, intellect or vital force. This you must understand.

That by whose proximity the body, the senses and other such objects acquire the power to act, to select and to differentiate —that am I. This you must understand.

That innermost Self which, changeless by nature, puts in motion the intellect and so forth, as the lodestone the iron —that am I. This you must understand.

The Self, the ultimate reality, in whose proximity the body, senses, mind and vital force, though by nature inert, appear to be conscious like the Self—that am I. This you must understand.

'My mind had moved elsewhere but now is still'. He who thus knows the mode of the mind—that am I. This you must understand.

He who cognizes the waking, dreaming and sleeping states of consciousness, who is immutable, who witnesses the presence and absence of objects—that am I. This you must understand.

He for whose sake alone song and wealth are loved, the Witness, the object of utmost endearment—that am I. This you must understand.

He who is the seer, who being the object of the highest love says: 'May I never suffer extinction! May I always exist!' —that am I. This you must understand."

THERE IS ONLY ONE SELF

The Self is the ultimate fact of our experience. The seemingly limited personality has to shed its individuality and be recognized as the all-pervasive infinite Self of all beings. For, contrary to common-sense belief, there is not a multiplicity of different selves but only one Self. This may be likened to a light shining through a number of prisms and refracting as different colours peculiar to each prism. The refracted light which takes on the colour of the prism is like the individual soul (jiva), which can thus be analysed into a real and an unreal element. In reality it is nothing but light, but it appears to take on certain limitations and characteristics of the medium through which it is refracted. Similarly, the individual soul (jiva) is in reality nothing but the Self (Atman or Brahman) but it appears to take on the limitations and characteristics of each personality and body in which it is 'refracted'. Because of this, the one Self, refracting through the medium of different personalities, comes to be regarded as many selves, but this is a mistake. The one-ness and all-pervasive nature of the Self is realized in the deep spiritual experience which may be termed super-consciousness, and which supersedes the ordinary waking consciousness as definitely as the latter supersedes dream.

At first our reason and experience protest against this idea. Our limited individuality seems so real; our neighbours and relatives seem so real, too, and to be quite distinct and set apart from us. Yet, if we think of it, all our experience is nothing but a stream of reports and impressions brought by the senses to the secluded monastery of our personality. The experiencer can never go outside himself, and the experiences all take place within his consciousness.

In this respect, is the waking experience so different from a dream? In a dream, a man may see himself driving through the countryside with a business acquaintance on the way to an important conference. The car, his friend, the scenery, the sense of urgency which springs from his having to reach the conference by a certain hour, and not least his own dream body and dream personality, seem extraordinarily real at the time; it is only when he wakes up that they are all recognized to have been modifications of his own consciousness. It is recorded that Dr. Johnson once dreamed that he was being worsted in debate by the orator Burke, and woke up in bed in a state of agitation and annoyance. On reflecting that he himself had been putting the arguments into Burke's mouth, he became calm once more and turned over happily. The Vedanta holds that troubles and suffering are due to the false belief that something exists other than one's Self, and that on 'waking up' to the Truth, the anxieties and sorrow which are a direct result of this false belief are at an end. To a knower of Self there is nothing outside himself which can be a cause of fear or suffering. As the verse of the Isha Upanishad asks:

"When to the knower all these objects are seen as the Self, what delusion or grief can there be when he sees this oneness?"

ADVAITA VEDANTA IS NOT PANTHEISM

In the Taittiriya Upanishad, Brahman is described as 'that fundamental Reality from which the world of beings is born, by which it is supported, and in which it finally dissolves'. Shri Shankara accepts the fact of the world from the standpoint of ordinary experience; he does not assert its complete unreality. The universes come into being, are sustained, and pass away like thoughts which momentarily rise to occupy the surface mind and then sink back into the sub-conscious. Brahman is the sole cause of the world, and the world is real only in so far as it is Brahman. According to Shri Shankara, the effect has no reality independent of its cause. The effect is a misreading of the cause. The world is Brahman wrongly interpreted.

This is not the doctrine of pantheism which either reduces the divine Existence to the level of worldly empirical existence or else deifies Nature and assigns to it the same position as God. The dream is only real in so far as it is part of the dreamer's consciousness. The dreamer is not only immanent in his dream-creation but he also transcends it. He is not affected by the changes which take place in the dream. God is not affected by the changes taking place in His creation; indeed, if He were, He would Himself be subject to eventual decay and death. He supports His creation, and yet also transcends it. In the Bhagavad Gita, the Incarnation of God, Shri Krishna, says: "I sustain this whole world by only a part of Myself".

MAYA

It may be asked: "If the Vedanta affirms that Brahman, the Reality, is non-dual and 'One-without-a-second' (advaita), how does the experience of the manifold world ever come about? How can the illusion, if so it be, ever begin?". Shri Shankara replies that it is due to Maya.

If a man tries to fix his eyes on the centre of the bright sun, he is dazzled and cannot see it. It is the extreme brilliance of the sun which covers it and prevents it from being seen. Similarly, it is the extreme luminosity of the supreme Consciousness which repels the intellect and does not allow it to identify itself with the Self. This is what is called Maya. Maya is not the antithesis of

Brahman; there is no duality in Brahman. But it is due to Maya that an apparent distinction exists between the world, the individual souls (jivas) and the personal God (Ishvara).

Maya is a power (shakti) of Brahman. It is something basically inexplicable and unaccountable which has its root in pure Consciousness. With His power of Maya, Brahman has projected the appearance of the world as time-space-causation just as a magician conjures up many strange forms by his magic power.

Questions about where, when and how the universe began can never be satisfactorily answered by the intellect because they already assume time, space and causation—that is, they already assume Maya. To seek to learn when time began is a philosophical absurdity. Being itself a product of Maya, the intellect can no more fathom the mystery of the origin of Maya than a son can be present at his father's christening. Within the dream, the history of the dream castles and personalities stretches back far into the unknown to a past which is beginningless.

If the intellect can never understand the workings of Maya, of which it is itself a tiny manifestation, it is even less able to reach a knowledge of Brahman through an analysis of Maya. An analysis of the dream only serves to give added reality to the dream and does not help to reveal the Sleeper. It is Maya's nature to conceal and to imprison the soul (jiva) by a web of ignorance; hence a synonym for Maya in the Vedanta is *ajnana* or *avidya* (nescience). Indicative of this characteristic is the common expression 'I do not know'; our knowledge of anything in the world only takes us so far, and then we find ourselves up against a brick wall. The limiting function of Maya also expresses itself as the bondage of the mind to ambition, pleasure-cravings, habits and prejudices which are allowed to grow up and dominate it. The yogic practices enable the soul to rise above the constrictions of Maya by encouraging it to withdraw interest from the passing phenomena and by refining the medium of the intellect to a pitch where the Self is no longer heavily obscured and can be realised in its true nature.

THE PERSONAL GOD (ISHVARA)

An important item of the yogic discipline is worship of the

personal God (Ishvara). Viewed in relation to His power of Maya
and its effect, the world, Brahman takes on the highest attributes
of Omniscience, Omnipotence, Truth and Love, and is
worshipped as the Creator and Sustainer of the Universe
(Ishvara). All analogies are imperfect, but as an illustration, if
Brahman is the blue sky, Ishvara is that part of the blue sky
on which the rainbow of the world is superimposed. The
intellect can know nothing of Brahman but it can have an idea
of Ishvara. Ishvara is the highest reading of Brahman by the
human mind, and it is Ishvara who, according to the Vedanta,
incarnates on earth from time to time out of compassion to turn
the minds of the deluded souls once more to the spiritual truths.
Not only Jesus Christ, but also Ramachandra, Krishna, Gautama
Buddha and others have been Incarnations of God on earth, and
an Incarnation under the name of Kalki is foretold for the future.

In the Indian rope trick, which is an illusion cast by a magician,
a figure is seen climbing up the rope to the sky. If that figure
were to become conscious and think itself to be independent
of its creator, it could only express wonder and admiration for
the magician. But such worship of the magician should ultimately
lead to the realisation that the magician is also the Self of the
figure and essentially untouched by the magic show which is
projected. Worship of the personal God is a great help in all
stages of Yoga. Prayer and meditation is a recognition that we
come from Him and are dependent on Him for every breath.
It is an opening of the heart to expose it to His light. Not to do
this and to blame God for the imperfections due to Maya is to
act like a bat which closes its eyes against the sunlight and
complains of the darkness. Ultimately the worship of Ishvara
is transformed into the realization of the unconditioned Brahman
beyond Maya and without attributes. The Mundaka Upanishad
says:

"The wise see That which is beyond perception, which is
incomprehensible, which has no origin, which is free from
all properties, which has neither the sense of hearing nor the
sense of perception, which has neither hands nor feet, which
is eternal, manifest in diversity, all-pervasive, extremely
subtle to grasp, imperishable, and the source of all beings".

THREE VIEWS OF MAYA

An object or a concept can be interpreted variously according to our measure of understanding. A child is attracted by a piece of coloured glass, which a jeweller recognises as a valuable diamond, and which a chemist would regard as a modification of carbon. These are three points of view about the same object. From the highest standpoint, Maya can be intuitively known to have no existence independent of Brahman—it is merely insufficiency of knowledge of Brahman. From the point of view of reason, Maya is inexplicable and alogical. It cannot be called absolutely real because it is changing and self-contradictory, nor can it be called absolutely unreal since it is experienced. Lastly, from the standpoint of the senses, Maya is an undeniable fact. It is important to understand that Shri Shankara does not hold the outer world to be an illusion in the sense of having a lesser degree of reality than the intellect which perceives it. Both outer world and perceiving intellect are as real as each other, but they are both part and parcel of Maya and are eventually to be recognized as unreal when Self-knowledge dawns, just as the dream personality and the dream objects lose their appearance of reality when the dreamer wakes up.

THE THREE BODIES

It has earlier been explained that the individual soul (jiva) is like the refraction of light conditioned and limited by a prism through which it passes. The personality and the body, which are products of Maya, give their own colouring to the light of the Spirit reflected in them. According to the simplest classification used in the Vedanta, the soul is encased in three bodies—the physical body, the mental body and the causal body. The causal body is the subtlest and innermost of the three bodies. Just as hydrogen and oxygen combine to form a pool of water, so the causal body gives rise to the other two bodies and pervades them as their subtle essence; in certain respects it is similar to the conception of the 'unconscious mind' in Western psychology. The mental body is roughly the mind or personality together with the life-force. The physical body is a grosser form of the mental substance, as ice is a grosser form of water.

THE PHYSICAL BODY

The physical body, composed of matter in its gross form, is easily identifiable and calls for no special comment. It is to be well cared-for by taking a sensible diet and reasonable physical exercise. The extremes of pampering the body through luxury and mortifying it through immoderate austerities are both to be avoided. Forms of exhibitionism such as lying on beds of spikes or squatting on poles have no spiritual value and are not sanctioned in the classics on Yoga. The Bhagavad Gita (VI 16/17) says:

"Yoga is impossible for the man who overeats or for the man who starves, or for the man who sleeps too much, or for the man who does not sleep enough. The Yoga which dispels sorrow is for the man who is temperate in his food, recreation, activity and sleep."

The specialized form of physical culture known as Hatha Yoga, which was a late development of certain schools, is not suited on the whole to living conditions in the West, and it can be dangerous unless it is accompanied by a strict discipline and is practised under the close supervision of an expert.

The classical Yoga regards the body as a useful instrument which needs to be kept in good condition. Perfect health is not an end in itself and is in any event like the crock of gold imagined at the bottom of a rainbow; the physical body, like everything in Maya, is subject to constant change, and perfect health, if it were attainable at all, could never be maintained for long.

THE MENTAL BODY

The mental body consists of the vital force (prana), whose chief manifestations are the breath and physical energy, together with the mind or personality. The mind is a covering of subtle matter which has spatial dimensions and operates in time. Inert by nature, the mind takes on the semblance of activity by reason of the reflection of the Spirit (Atman) in it which, so to say, energizes it. Although the mind always acts as a unified whole, four main aspects of it may be distinguished. These are intellect (buddhi), ego (ahankara), lower mind (manas) and memory (chitta).

INTELLECT (BUDDHI)

The word "buddhi" comes from a root meaning "to awaken" or "to be awake to" and is the mental faculty through which a man is awake to the significance of his acts. The powers of reasoning, decision and determination are characteristics of the intellect, which is also the seat of the awareness of right and wrong and the sense of moral responsibility. It is for the intellect to understand and interpret experience, to resolve on a course of action and to direct the emotional drives.

EGO (AHANKARA)

Ahankara is the sense of 'I'. It is like the nucleus of dust around which a drop of water condenses or like the centre of a whirlpool. All the experiences of the mind are 'owned' by this little 'I'. In the moral sphere, it is the source of egoism and the instinct for self-preservation.

LOWER MIND (MANAS)

The lower mind is like a gatekeeper standing at the gate of the senses. During a man's waking hours, a myriad impressions of sight, sound, touch, taste and smell are all the time battering for admission. The lower mind admits only certain of these impressions and rejects the rest. It also co-ordinates the impressions received so that, for instance, the sight and scent of a rose are synthesised in the single impression of a rose which is presented to the intellect.

MEMORY (CHITTA)

An important stage in the identification and evaluation of any sense-impression is reference to the store of past memories and experiences. Every thought and experience is registered on the mental fabric as if filed away in a permanent library in the basement of the mind. Chitta is this library, and the past impressions and mental images which it contains are called *vasanas* or *sanskaras*. As occasion offers, chitta throws up these latent impressions in the form of memories and impulses. Also, when any new impression is received through the senses, it is identified (and often enriched) by being checked against the stock of past impressions of the same type in the chitta. For example, the impression of a sunset is received through the sense of sight; it is identified and evaluated through being compared with the memories of previous sunsets which have been seen. This happens so quickly that more often than not it is not a conscious process, but reflection will show that something of this sort must have happened.

MIND FUNCTIONS AT TWO LEVELS

Manas and chitta are together regarded as mind functioning on a lower level, whereas buddhi and ahankara combine the higher functions. The former pair represent the largely negative response to outer stimuli while the latter stand for the positive acts of knowing, willing, enjoying and so on, in which every psychological process culminates. Detailed analyses of them are given, particularly in the later writers on Vedanta, and the main fact which they illustrate is that all mental functions, such as will and the emotional tendencies of love and hate, can manifest at different levels and with varying intensity. As a simple example, the 'selection' of one sense-impression rather than another by the lower mind—let us say when the eyes are attracted by a striking detail in a large canvas by an old master—implies preference (like) for the one and rejection (dislike) of the remainder; it is an act which reproduces on an elementary plane what would be recognized at the level of intellect as a 'decision' following an emotional reaction of assent or dissent.

For the student of Yoga, the moral and spiritual struggle centres round the mind, which can either be an enemy of the soul and a means of binding it to the phenomenal world and a life of suffering, or can become a friend and a help to the bliss of God-vision. The practices of Yoga are aimed at persuading the mind to abdicate from the throne which it has usurped and at reconciling it to its rightful position of a useful and willing servant.

THE CAUSAL BODY

The innermost and most subtle layer of the personality is the causal body. While the physical body is most active in the waking state, and the mind has its greatest play in the world of dream and phantasy, dreamless sleep is the characteristic state of the causal body. It is the undifferentiated form of Maya in which all the potentialities of the mind lie in seed form until they sprout forth at the time of dream and waking.

The causal body is also referred to as 'the sheath of bliss'. Since it is the most subtle veil of matter, the Self (Atman), which is Bliss by nature, reflects more clearly in it than in the more opaque medium of the mind, and hence happiness is experienced. The experience of happiness in the waking and dream states occurs when the mind is temporarily tranquillized, perhaps owing to the satisfaction of a desire which had been agitating it; such a temporary stilling of the mind enables the soul to have a glimpse of the bliss of Self reflected in the causal body. The relaxed contentment of dreamless sleep is held to be the happiest condition experienced by the soul in Maya.

THE LINK BETWEEN MICROCOSM AND MACROCOSM

An important thesis of Vedanta is that the characteristics observed in the microcosm are also reproduced in the cycles and sub-cycles of the macrocosm. For instance, the universe in which we now live—and which is only one of a large number of universes which have been created in the past and are still to be created—comes into manifestation, remains in existence for a certain period, and will then be withdrawn into the undifferentiated state of Maya which may be likened to the cosmic causal body of God (Ishvara). On the same pattern, an individual's mental activity starts at the beginning of the day and continues until the evening, when it is once more absorbed in the causal body during dreamless sleep. Again, the rise of a single thought, its retention by the mind for a short time, and its eventual fall back into the sub-conscious is the same process working on a yet smaller scale.

THE THREE GUNAS

Running through microcosm and macrocosm, like the threads of which a cloth is woven, are the three 'constituents' (gunas) of Maya, known as *sattva*, *rajas* and *tamas*. The Bhagavad Gita says (18.40):

"There is no creature on earth or again in heaven among the
Gods who is free from the three gunas of Maya."

Rajas guna typifies activity in all its forms whereas tamas demon-
strates the opposite tendency of inertia. Sattva guna stands for
balance, purity, light and peace. Everything in the world,
material and psychological, inner and outer, is pervaded by the
gunas and can be classified according to the predominating guna.
Though necessarily incomplete, the following table illustrates
the manifestation of the three gunas in the outer world and in
the inner world of the mind:—

	SATTVA	RAJAS	TAMAS
EXTERNAL WORLD	Light	Life	Darkness
	Balance	Force	Mass
	Order	Movement	Inertia
MIND	Happiness	Desire	Fear
	Equanimity	Restlessness	Laziness
	Balanced judgment	Passion	Stupidity

The state of society and international relations simply reflect
the inner condition of man. Wars and strife are the externali-
zation of inner conflicts. Thus the betterment of society and the
maintenance of peace between nations, according to the Yoga,
depend less upon economic and political moves than upon men
establishing inner harmony in their own minds by the cultivation
of sattva, in other words by first becoming "at peace with
themselves".

The veil of Maya, which obscures the true nature of the Self,
is so to speak thinnest where sattva predominates, and conversely
is thickest where tamas predominates. Tamas conceals the Self
as if under a heavy quilt; rajas does so by throwing up dis-
tractions and agitations which engage the attention of the soul.
Emphasis is therefore laid on the cultivation of purity of the
mind by ethical discipline, without which the practice of Yoga
is of no more use than trying to fill a bottle with water by holding
it upside down under a tap.

ETHICS

Although Self-knowledge—and not ethics—is the goal of life, ethical discipline is considered essential for the realization of that goal. The Katha Upanishad (2. 24) says:

"No-one who has not turned away from evil conduct, whose senses are not controlled, whose mind is not concentrated and tranquillized, can attain this Self by knowledge."

Ethical discipline enables a man to break with the animal side of his nature, which is continually urging him to satisfy lower desires, and to transcend the irrational feelings of attachment and aversion. Only in this way is the attainment of spiritual vision (moksha) made possible. And when his final purpose is achieved, the Sage still continues to be one "who is ever engaged in furthering the good of all" (Bhagavad Gita, V.25).

The Upanishads contain many ethical injunctions such as:
"Speak the truth; follow righteousness."
"Let thy parents be a God to thee; let thy Teacher be a God to thee; let the uninvited guest be a God to thee."
"Truth alone prevails, never falsehood."
"Do not covet the wealth of others."

The Bhagavad Gita and other textbooks of Yoga give detailed ethical instruction which accords with the very similar teachings of the authors of Christianity, Buddhism and other great religions.

Evil conduct springs from the sense of egoism; its motive is always personal self-interest. Virtue (dharma) is an attitude which denies egoism by looking upon the good of others as synonymous with one's own good. A modern saint, Swami Rama Tirtha, has said: "Egoism is the cork on the bottle; remove the cork and let the personal consciousness fly free and expand to infinity". This is an echo of a verse in one of Shri Shankaracharya's best-known shorter works *The Crest-Jewel of Discrimination*:

"With the cessation of selfish action, brooding on sense-objects is stopped and this leads to the elimination of desires. The elimination of desires is liberation (moksha)."

Desires agitate the mind as the wind rustles the surface of a pool
so that the reflection of the sun in the pool is distorted and lost
to sight. The Self can only be realized when the mind is serene
and unagitated by desires, and ethical conduct is the means to
bring this about. A verse of the Katha Upanishad sums it up:

"When all desires dwelling in the heart are destroyed, then
the mortal becomes immortal and he attains Brahman even
here in this life."

ACTION (KARMA)

Action is the key to the ethical life. Many of the early Christians,
like St. Anthony, regarded action as a hindrance to the spiritual
life and sought to escape from it in a life of monasticism. The
view of Yoga is that action is only the instrument of change,
which is the nature of Maya, and that man cannot avoid action
for a single moment. Even in sleep physiological changes are
going on in the body, and the mind is functioning to a certain
extent. Action in itself is neither a help nor a hindrance to the
attainment of God-vision but it can become either according to
the use made of it.

Apart from certain actions which are ethically neutral such as
the physiological functions of breathing and walking, all
purposive action is either good or bad; that is to say, it either
accelerates or retards the soul's progress towards liberation
(moksha). "As a man thinks, so he becomes" is the maxim of
Yoga. Thought materializes in action and shapes not only the
character of the thinker but also his future environment and
circumstances. If we do good deeds, our minds are lightened
and expanded, circumstances will bring us into touch with the
teaching of the great religions, and we shall have a desire to be
liberated. If we do bad deeds, we shall eventually suffer for
them and shall continue to remain blind to the spiritual facts.
Good actions are those which are untainted by selfish motives
and which cause no suffering to others. The Sage is one who
"does not afflict the world and is not afflicted by it." Selfish action
is bad action; certainly no-one can be happy who causes suffering and unhappiness to other people.

The law of karma is that we reap what we sow. To this extent we are architects of our fate. Our present surroundings and opportunities are the result of our previous actions—not only in this life but in many past lives—while our reactions to these surroundings and the use we make of the opportunities will condition our lives in the future. Even in a small way, if a married couple keep their house clean and attractive, establish a harmonious atmosphere and entertain their friends open-handedly, they create favourable conditions for themselves and draw congenial company towards them. The opposite is true of the miserly fellow who squats in the dust of his home, scarcely ever going out and making no contribution to the good of others. His plight, which is of his own making in the first instance, binds his soul, and the longer it persists the more difficult it becomes for him to break free; the compassion of a good man may be the only means of his doing so.

DEATH AND REINCARNATION

The Yoga holds that the soul returns to the world in a new body after death and will continue to do so until it has reached the goal of spiritual evolution called liberation (moksha). There is a verse in the Bhagavad Gita (II, 22):

"As a man casts off worn-out clothes and puts on new ones, so does the incarnated soul leave its worn-out bodies and enter new ones."

After death, the physical body returns to its constituent elements like a candle that has burnt itself out. The causal and mental bodies, which contain the store of all past experiences, are preserved and continue to act as a prism in which the light of the Self (Atman) reflects as the individual soul (jiva). It is therefore the causal and mental bodies and the individual soul which "reincarnates", and not the real Self (Atman).

On leaving the body after death, the soul may "go to" Heaven or Hell, but these are taken to be temporary states in which the desires conceived while in the body are realized in the form of a dream. For example, a Christian who has been devoted to the Lord of Galilee will be rewarded by a vision of Him and his soul will be flooded with light and bliss. A devout Hindu will find himself welcomed at the court of Shri Ramachandra, and a Mohammedan will go to his Paradise. On the other hand, a man of uncontrollable and insatiable appetites in this world will find himself in a "Hell" of burning desires which he is unable to satisfy. These Heavens and Hells of various kinds do not last for ever, and when the karmic merit or demerit which has warranted these experiences has been exhausted, the soul takes birth once again in a human body.

LIBERATION (MOKSHA)

The process of birth, death and re-birth is not endless. It lasts only so long as man has not consciously realized the truth of the saying:

"God is real, the world is illusory,
The individual soul and God are one and the same."

The possession of a human body and mind already marks substantial progress in the spiritual evolution of the soul, which has earlier had innumerable plant and animal bodies. It is with this instrument—and only with this instrument—that the soul can be liberated from the bondage of Maya. 'God-realization' or 'Self-realization' is a term often used because it does not imply knowing something new but rather recognizing what is already a fact. The teachers of Yoga tell the story of a lion cub who was left in the forest soon after birth when its parents were shot by a party of hunters. The cub grew up with a flock of wild sheep and, since it saw nothing but sheep around it, thought itself also to be a sheep. One day it caught sight of its reflection in a clear pool of water and, giving a roar for the first time in its life, threw off its meekness and knew itself to be a king of the jungle. The Yoga says that man is like that lion cub. He is ever the God-Self (Brahman) but imagines himself to be a helpless individual doomed to a life of frustration and disappointment only occasionally relieved by some brighter moments. At any time he can see his reflection in his refined and tranquillized mind and realize the lion-like majesty of his Self. At the right moment the teacher will say to him: "Tat tvam asi! (That thou art!). Thou, the individual soul, art in truth the supreme Reality (Brahman)", and the consciousness will break: "Aham Brahmasmi! (I am Brahman)". This realization can come before the death of the body in this life. Such liberation in life is known as jivanmukti, and the one who is so liberated is called a jivanmukta. A jivanmukta is in perpetual bliss and enjoys the play of the phenomenal world rising and falling in his own consciousness. Such a jivanmukta, the Saint Nirbhayanandaji, recorded his experience in these lines:

"O Nirbhaya, my boat has crossed the strong sea.
My Guru has opened my eyes.
Knowing how wonderful is Maya in all its hallucinations and illusions,
I laugh and laugh and laugh, and keep time with the beat of my mind,
Enjoying Maya instead of being afraid of it."

In the next chapter we shall consider the methods through which this discovery of Truth, peace and bliss within the Self can be made.

3

THE PRACTICE OF YOGA

THE practice of Yoga has two parts: practice in the special meditation period each day, and practice outside that period in everyday life. The practice in everyday life clears the mind and purifies it; the special meditation practice focusses the clarified mind and makes it perfectly still. In meditation the purified and motionless mind is focussed towards the supreme Reality, at first conceived as something unknown and ·distant. When meditation reaches its culmination, the illusory limitations of body and even of mind drop off, and the Self of man is known to be one with that Reality. At the beginning the supreme Reality is conceived with the aid of a traditional symbol, such as the Sun, which gives to the questing mind some idea of glory and infinity, but in the end these limitations of time and space also drop off. In the Isha Upanishad the sage meditates at the beginning: "O sun, withdraw thy blinding rays, that I may see the Reality which is within thee." When his meditation is complete, his experience is: "O I know, He that is within thee is within me also." All differences melt away, and the Self of man is known and felt to be the Self of the universe also.

SUBJECTS FOR MEDITATION

According to the sage Patanjali, one of the authorities, there are six main classes of things to meditate on. We should find texts in the scriptures or writings of great sages which treat of these things, and meditate on them.

1. *Peace of Mind*. We create first feelings of universal friendliness and compassion for the unhappy and the unrighteous. This leads us to meditation on Peace of Mind.

Devotion to the Lord is one of the quickest means of calming the mind. "On knowing Me, the Lord of all sacrifices and austerities, the great Lord of all worlds, the Friend of all beings, he attains Peace" (Bhagavad Gita, V. 29).

Those who do not believe in God may sit still and, breathing normally, count the breaths for a few minutes. The counting produces a certain amount of tranquillity, and they then go deeper into peace by meditating on universal friendliness and compassion. The Buddhist yogis have a sutra on breath-counting, and some of the lower yogas make much of concentration on breath; but in the classical yoga it is only a preliminary practice, to be dispensed with as the power of meditation increases.

2. *The true Self, shining and beyond all limitations.* To practise this meditation it is necessary to have studied an outline of the philosophy of Yoga, otherwise the mind can never rest in it. It seems opposed to our common sense to say that the Self is beyond all limitations, and it *is* opposed to common sense. But common sense only means our experience so far. Common sense tells a child that the earth is flat, but when he has seen a ship disappearing beneath the horizon at sea he gives up his old idea and accepts the new truth. The yogic philosophy will show us that the infinity of the Self is not an unreasonable theory, and it is for us to test in practice whether it is true or not.

Some meditation texts on the true Self are:

"My self is pure consciousness, calm and infinite, like the waveless ocean". (Shri Vyasa's commentary on Patanjali)

"That God who is the Self in all, impersonal and changeless, like unto space, by nature purity itself, verily, verily, that am I". (Avadhut Gita)

"I am the honey of existence, I am the sun. I am the ancient sage, I the first man". (Upanishad)

"Ye are Gods". (Psalm 82)

"Before Abraham was, I am".

"I and the Father are one".

"Be ye perfect even as the Father is perfect". (Holy Bible)

"Know that Allah is nearer than the neck-vein". (Holy Koran)

These meditations are like reviving the memory in a man who has lost it. He is given his real name by the doctor and repeats it with conviction. He is shown pictures of his house and relatives and friends, and tries to remember them. His mind says: "I do not know these people", but through repetition with conviction his memory comes back, first in flashes and fragments, and then completely. The memory is not just the idea: "Well, I do know them after all" (that could be merely auto-suggestion), but a living experience which brings with it all the associated memories of incidents in childhood and so on quite unknown to the doctor. In the meditation we reject the agitation of the mind which doubts the infinity of the Self and asserts its limitation. Slowly this agitation dies down. Like a small child which strips off its clothes one by one to run naked in the sunlight, so we strip off the convictions 'I am this body', 'I am old, I am sick', 'I am sad', 'I am angry', 'I am this mind, I am so-and-so', and come naked into the sunlight of Infinity.

The Upanishads say that no human joy is more than a pale reflection compared with the infinite bliss of realization of the true Self.

3. *An Incarnation, or great sage.* The lives of the Incarnations of the Lord should be studied in the scriptures such as the Gospels (especially the Fourth Gospel), the Ramayana, the devotional poems of Surdas and others, the Buddhist scriptures (the *Light of Asia* of Sir Edwin Arnold is an excellent life of Buddha) and so on. The stories of the Incarnations have a peculiar charm and reveal newer and newer meanings when studied repeatedly. A vivid mental picture of the Incarnation will be created by this kind of study, and the meditator should visualize the Lord teaching His disciples and himself sitting in reverence and peace among them.

If not an Incarnation, then the lives of great sages may be studied. Socrates, Confucius, Bodhidharma, Mohammed and their great successors all lived for universality and self-realization. By an intense application to their lives and meditation on their form and their heart, their great qualities begin to appear in the meditator.

4. *Dream and Sleep.* In our ordinary lives we live mainly in illusion and can be compared to dreaming people. It is necessary to study the philosophy of Yoga and understand the nature of

the illusion and the process of waking up. Briefly, it is our passionate hopes and fears, based on the conviction of the reality of the world, that support the illusion in our waking life just as it is our conviction of its reality that supports the dream. In the dream our hopes of wealth and fears of destruction will never be realized because they are unreal. By deep meditation we should understand that this is true of the waking world also. The aim of this meditation is to secure detachment and freedom from unconscious compulsions and habits. The world is not absolutely unreal; it has *some* reality behind it, but we cannot know its true reality while we are desperately clinging to the false appearances of things.

5. *Vital currents of the body.* This is a subsidiary meditation. Press the forefinger between the eyebrows, and draw it down the centre line of the body lightly, over the nose, lips, throat, breast, to the navel. Now fold the hands and put the attention on to this line, using the sensation caused by the pressure as an aid to begin. Shut the eyes and think of it as a line of light down the centre of the body. At the beginning it is only an imagination, but there is a line of light here and it is known as the meditation advances. This practice calms the mind.

6. *OM.* This is one of the greatest and highest meditations. OM (pronounce to rhyme with HOME) is a word of no known language, revered in nearly all the mystical schools of the world. It is the highest name of God. It stands for the supreme Truth. It is infinite consciousness and bliss. The inner meanings can be studied in the Mandukya Upanishad and other texts. All meditations can be summed up in OM. Peace of mind is OM, the supreme Self is OM, the Incarnations and sages are OM, the waking, dreaming and sleeping states and the state of liberation from all of them are OM, the vital currents of the body are OM.

All meditation and mystic practices should begin and end with one or more repetitions of "OM", uttered with great reverence; by this obstacles are removed, mistakes are rectified, and many advantages follow.

Fig. 1. OM

The symbol OM is the highest name of God and is used in many of the mystic schools. It is sometimes explained as a representation of the individual and Divine Consciousness which are in essence identical. The lower curve, which is the longest, represents the waking state. The upper curve represents the state of dreamless sleep. The curve springing from the junction of these two represents the dreaming condition. The semi-circle with the dot represents the state of liberation which is beyond the other three states; the circle is left incomplete to signify infinity. Repetition of OM and meditation on OM are valued in Yoga as a potent means of awakening the spiritual centres in the personality.

PRACTICE IN DAILY LIFE

The moral discipline laid down by all the yogis is summarized by Patanjali as follows: goodwill towards all, irrespective of class or colour; telling the truth; not stealing; control of the sex impulse; not being enslaved by the things of the world; purity, external and internal; contentment, being neither over-elated in success nor crushed by failure; austerity; study; devotion to the Supreme Lord or simply to Truth.

The principle behind this discipline is that our acts and strong emotions make impressions in the roots of the mind, and these impressions will germinate like seeds, sometimes years later when the act or feeling has been forgotten. If the hidden impressions are based on conviction of the absolute reality of the world and passionate attachment to it or fear of it, then they will arise to disturb our meditation and prevent our knowledge of truth. But those impressions caused by acts and feelings based on universality, and directed towards the Reality which underlies the apparent world, will not hinder the meditation, because they do not emphasize the separate "I", but tend to dissolve it in the universal "I", which is God.

The discipline arises naturally when we become more and more convinced that there is the same supreme Self hidden in all beings. Common sense should be used in deciding in any particular case what is our duty; we should do those actions which serve and elevate other beings, doing them purely as a service to the Lord in them, and we should avoid those actions and thoughts which degrade us in our own eyes.

The last three items of the discipline, study, devotion, and austerity, can be explained briefly here. *Study* means primarily reading or hearing the great scriptures and the writings of teachers of all ages and countries. There should be no narrowness. Truth must be sought in every quarter, say both St. Thomas Aquinas and the prophet Mohammed. But it is worthwhile taking one book for our chief study for a few months, and trying to go deeper and deeper into its thought. The great inspired writings only reveal their true meaning after repeatedly and sincerely applying the mind to them. *Devotion to the Lord* means to offer all our actions to Him as a sacrifice, and to free ourselves from all fear and dependence on the world by taking refuge in Him. Those who are not religious must free themselves from dependence and fear by reverence for truth and by realizing the illusory nature of the world by analysis.

Austerity means to loose ourselves from unnecessary habits and love of comfort. To fast one day a month, occasionally to sit up three hours in the night studying and meditating, to train ourselves not to be too much affected by heat and cold—these are some typical examples of what is called tapas (austerity). We should apply common sense here too; it is useless undertaking such a severe tapas that it harms our health. But again it is no use ruling out all tapas on this excuse or that; every yogi has to undertake some physical tapas.

The other form of austerity is the austerity of thought, and this is one of the most important practices of Yoga, absolutely essential for the final Illumination. During the day, when we have two or three minutes to spare, we must practise dropping our present current of thought and taking up one of the yogic thoughts. After a predetermined time, say three minutes, or perhaps the time taken to walk down the street we are in, we should drop the yogic thought and can again return to the worldly thoughts. Ultimately the yogic thoughts will appear of themselves, as a background to our mental life. This practice is not so difficult as it may appear. If we examine our everyday minds, we find them full of odds and ends—we are endless humming a snatch of a popular song or repeating some almost meaningless phrase. Instead of this valueless ragbag, we may as well have as the background of our mind the yogic visions of universality and illumination, which permanently ennoble the mind and soul.

Some people may say: "Oh, if we are trying to think about Yoga all the time, we shall not be able to play our part in life." It is not so. First of all, as has been explained, there *is* already a constant background to our directed and conscious thought, and that background as it is now is often a great disadvantage in life because it is sometimes a nagging worry or energy-consuming pose. We can change this background for a helpful one. Second, we know of many cases in which clear and conscious thoughts are kept in the background of the mind without interfering with daily life. Take the spy who sets up a business in a foreign capital. He is interested in his business and does well at it; but all the time at the back of his mind is the hidden objective. Again, a mother who goes out to work, leaving her baby in the care of a neighbour, works well but always has the thought of the baby in her mind. In exactly the same way the yogi retains the subject of meditation as a background even in his worldly activity, and as a matter of fact this practice relieves many of the tensions and anxieties of worldly life.

PRACTICE AT THE SPECIAL MEDITATION PERIOD

In the solitude of your own room, or in another quiet place, set aside about half an hour every day, at the same time, for the special yogic practices. At this time a determined effort is made to see right through the veils of illusion, namely the conviction of the absolute reality of the world and the feeling of identity with our individual body and mind, to the Reality which underlies the universe. That Reality is the same as the Reality within us, beyond body and mind. The meditation process is to still, relax and finally altogether forget the body, to still and to concentrate the mind first on a text or form taken as a symbol, and then expand it to infinity. Mind too is forgotten and the true Self, the Reality beyond the mind, blazes forth like the sun coming out as the clouds dissolve.

Posture. Meditation is best practised in a sitting posture, and experience has shown that there is an advantage in sitting on the floor. Among the traditional postures are those shown in Figures 2 and 3. Few Europeans can sit comfortably for long as shown in Fig. 2, but students under thirty can attain the other position in a few weeks by practising ten minutes night and morning. The attainment of the posture is made easier by putting a small cushion or folded rug under the hips, to raise them slightly. It is not necessary to achieve these postures fully (if it were, a one-legged man could not succeed in Yoga), but something like them should be aimed at—that is, spine erect, head balanced on the spine, the upper body balanced on the loins, muscles relaxed and the weight of the body taken on the bones. "Posture becomes perfect through relaxation and meditation on the infinite", says Patanjali. When appreciable progress has been made in meditation, small defects in the posture will remedy themselves.

In cases of illness or where the upright posture is not possible, the student may lie flat on a blanket on the floor, with no pillow.

The student should not shift his posture during the meditation. It will be found helpful before meditation to stretch the limbs

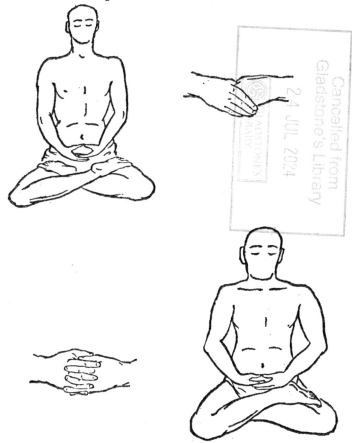

Figs. 2 and 3.   MEDITATION POSTURES

and trunk. The student may observe and imitate the stretching of a cat or dog when it gets up from sleep.

Meditation may also be practised, within the limits that

common sense lays down, when walking or standing, and experts practise a form of meditation all the time. But there are many advantages in learning the traditional meditation technique at the beginning.

Pranayama. Pranayama means "control of the vital currents". It is one of the preliminary practices recommended both for lethargic and for nervous people.

Sit in the meditation posture in relaxation, and breathe in and out slowly, very slowly; the breaths should be as full as can be comfortably managed. Do this five times. Do not hold the breath at all. This is the first part of the exercise. Now in the same posture, without moving, breathe normally and count the breaths (as described under Subjects for Meditation), for ten minutes. This practice makes the mind alert but peaceful. Then go on to the meditation proper.

Pranayama is like the water-wings given to a beginner in swimming; they lift his head a little out of the water and make it easier for him to try the strokes. A great fuss has been made by some schools of pseudo-yoga in the West over elaborate systems of Pranayama. But these complicated systems, which traditionally require isolation from the world and a very restricted diet, are of doubtful value for attaining illumination and freedom in daily life. It is like giving bigger and bigger water-wings to the beginner; they lift him out of the water a bit more and may give him a false feeling of achievement, but he never learns to swim, and if they should be punctured, he is lost.

The same applies to many other physical exercises and practices on the fringes of Yoga, such as Mula-bandha (fundamental control). The advantages they give at the beginning are largely illusory, because we have to learn to do without them in the end. Shri Shankara, the greatest authority on the true Yoga of the Upanishads and the Gita, makes it quite clear in his Aparok-shanubhuti that by the mere practice of meditation all the accessories—posture, Pranayama, and other controls—will come about naturally themselves, and until the meditation has ripened, too much effort to produce these things by themselves is pointless. It is like tying artificial roses on to the rose tree; they soon drop off. But if the tree is nourished and looked after properly, it will produce its own true roses which are far more beautiful and lasting.

Withdrawal. The Sanskrit word is Pratyahara, which means withdrawal or rejection. In grammar, if out of a whole list of words we select just one group, rejecting all the others, that is called a Pratyahara, and this gives us a clue to its meaning in meditation practice. At the chosen time, in a quiet place, we sit in the meditation posture and calm the mind and nerves by a little Pranayama. Now we present the text (or other object) of meditation to the mind, reading it three times, then shutting the eyes and trying to go into it.

Immediately a host of other thoughts, memories, emotions, urgent duties that must be performed at once, and so on will flood into the mind. We shall have difficulty in keeping the meditation before us. Now we are introduced to one of the great laws of Yogic mental control: *No thought can remain long in the mind unless we actively support it with our vital energy.* As each irrelevant thought arises, we meet it with "Not wanted" and turn away our attention. We should not become angry at its persistence, nor in any way acknowledge its right to enter our mind. We must not argue with the thoughts or elaborate on them. They are like pigeons whom we have fed every day; now they come as usual for their food, and if we do not give it, they make a clamour. They fly round in agitation and try to attract our attention. If we shout at them they become encouraged, feeling that they have at least secured that. But we must leave the window closed and all silent within. If we do it day after day, they become discouraged and go to seek for food elsewhere.

This is the process of Pratyahara, and to master it is a great advantage in life, not only in Yoga. To be able to think what we like, instead of being the prey of any wandering thought and the hypnotised victim of any orator who wishes to exploit us, is true freedom, and without it no political system can give its people any real freedom at all.

Concentration. The Sanskrit word is Dharana, which means

to uphold or support. For some time, when we present the
object of meditation to the mind, we have the experience that
it soon fades away. If it is a text, the words seem to be of little
meaning; if we meditate on a form, it becomes vague. At other
times the meditation is disturbed by restlessness, by wondering
how we are getting on, by doubts as to the validity of the process
and so on. A good deal depends at this stage on the study which
we have put in. Just as a dog cannot settle down in a new home
until he has explored it thoroughly, so the mind cannot settle
down into a meditation until a good deal of study has been put
into it. Study shows us that the conclusion of the meditation is
not unreasonable; it sets our restless doubts at rest. Of course
study alone can not prove the truth contained in the meditation;
but it can convince us that what we are trying to do is worth
while.

By tapas (austerity), especially the austerity of thought
described in the previous pages, and by devotion, concentration
is strengthened. While we are practising concentration, we should
be very patient. Again and again the text of meditation is dropped
by our wavering mind, and again and again we pick it up and
revive it without fuss or disturbance. Slowly a current of interest
is created, and now the concentration becomes easier and more
natural. Suppose we meditate on the text:

"In the early morning,
I bow to him who dwells beyond darkness,
Who shines as the sun;
In him,
We, peering through this veil of darkness,
Imagine that we see the universe brought forth,
Even as, in darkness,
Men think a rope a snake".

The mind says: "No, the world is real, and God, if the word
has any meaning at all, is only a creation of man's fears or hopes".
"If he is real, why do we not see him?" Such questions will arise
endlessly unless we have studied. But study will tell us to consider
the case of a dream. There is the sleeper, who nowhere appears

in the dream, and yet in him the mountains, rivers, and people of the dream are imagined as brought forth. Going deeper, we find that the sleeper has created a tiny replica of himself who appears in the dream, and enjoys and suffers from the imaginary objects of the dream. If we say to a man in a nightmare, dreaming of a storm at sea: "All these things, ship, waves, howling winds, are no more than appearances in you", he will think the words ridiculous. But still, if his attention is directed away from the dream into his own self, he finds that the true self is not bound by the limitations of the dream-body and dream-mind, but contains the storm and everything in it. Study tells us that the waking world is in this respect (though not in every way) comparable to a dream, and shows us that it is reasonable to suppose that we can awaken to the Reality behind it. Meditation is the actual experiment, the direct and living confirmation, but our mind will never be steady enough to meditate unless we understand what we are trying to do. Let us understand that just as the dreaming man can never be nourished by eating the food in the dream, nor become wealthier by gaining its riches, nor be killed by its storm, so all our fears in this world are ultimately illusory and our possessions of no value, unless we know the Reality in the universe and in our own Self.

Contemplation (*Dhyana*). In concentration (Dharana) there is always a certain effort to bridge over the lapses of attention, but in the next stage, Dhyana (rather provisionally translated as "contemplation"), the flow of thought on the object is continuous, without any break or distraction. The poor man who finds a precious jewel which will make him rich hides it in a cupboard in his shop; all day he has it in mind, and though attending to his business he always keeps an eye on the cupboard. But in the evening, when all have gone to bed and the house is silent, he takes it out and looks silently at it, lost in its beauty and power. This is a form of Dhyana, but because the object is something limited in time and space, it is always liable to be lost or destroyed, and so the Dhyana is to some extent a meditation on narrowness and fear. As such it does not lead to truth or ultimate joy.

The Dhyana of the Yoga is an uninterrupted flow of thought towards something which symbolizes infinity. All the limitations of the ego as well as of the object begin to be transcended. "I bow to him, the Self, who dwells beyond darkness, Who shines as the sun . . ." "I bow" means here that the separate ego, identified with body and mind, annihilates itself before the grand vision of unity, the Consciousness which contains the whole universe. Then that Consciousness is found in the individual also, where it had been merely concealed by the false ego, as the sun by a thick cloud.

When contemplation (Dhyana) is reached, the words of the texts take on a new meaning, the things of the world take on a new significance.

Samadhi. In Samadhi we reach the very roots of the mind; the last veils are dissolved that separate the Consciousness encased in the limited body and mind and the Consciousness that underlies the whole universe. Subject and object of the meditation become one. The thought "I am meditating" is also lost. This is a state beyond the operations of the mind, and the mind can give no description of it. The sages have given us hints and allusions to it, but they can be no more than that.

"The one cause of all misery and suffering is that by your thought or action you make the world real and God (Truth) unreal. The one cure is to make God real and know the world to be unreal. Suppose you face a great disaster, but you do your daily meditation and do not cheat the Lord in it—again and again you rise above your body consciousness and you meditate on 'I have splendour like the sun, the sun is my abode'—then every anxiety and worry of yours will be burnt to ashes". (Swami Rama Tirtha)

In Samadhi there is no effort; the efforts were made in the austerity of thought in daily life, and in Dharana and Dhyana. Some mystics say that it is the Grace of the Lord that gives Samadhi. This is another way of saying that in the high states of Dhyana the God within, who is the same as the God without, begins to awaken and in Samadhi Himself throws off the last quilts that covered His Majesty and glory.

In Samadhi the limitations of the individual consciousness fall off—the limitations being of the form "I am this body, this mind, limited by time, space and death, and subject to transformation." All memories, desires and so on are discarded.

If a man takes something finite as the object of meditation, and goes into Samadhi in his meditation, it is a lower Samadhi; it reveals, says Patanjali, the truth about that object But it is not the high Samadhi and does not reveal the ultimate truth. He is not speaking here of trivialities, but of a revelation of the cosmic laws. Professor Yukawa, the Japanese physicist who won the Nobel prize for Physics for his prediction of the particle called the meson, said that the new idea came to him when he was alone, late at night, and he had passed into a state of meditation on the problem. Newton, too, passed into meditation states in which he was totally insensible to the world around him. Many artists speak of such experiences as the source of their inspiration.

But Pantanjali makes it clear that meditation on anything finite will not give release from the illusions and consequent sufferings of worldly life. To be attached to any worldly success that may come as a result of the lower Samadhi strengthens the bonds of ignorance, and then it will become increasingly difficult to throw them off and enter again into Samadhi.

The true Samadhi is to meditate on the infinity within the object of meditation, until the limited ego is lost in the majesty and glory which are revealed, or else to meditate on the infinity within the mind itself. In the second case the ego as it were expands to infinity, becoming the self of all beings and of the whole universe. In one case the universal Lord is meditated upon as without, in the other case as within, but the end is the same— "I am He."

LIBERATION IN LIFE

When the yogi enters into Samadhi, he attains unity with the Infinite Self that is behind the whole universe. His body and mind do not remain eternally in meditation. They come out of meditation, but they are now the direct instruments of the Lord. The actions and thoughts of the yogi are not centred round the individuality, as are those of the ordinary man. His action and thought are directed towards universal good, are inspired by universal truth and create beauty of a universal kind. This does not mean that all liberated yogis are great artistic geniuses; but their very lives are poems—structures of perfect beauty. However, where there is artistic or other talent it often blossoms into genius at the touch of Samadhi. Nearly all the great poets, painters, musicians, philosophers, and even statesmen of the East have been students of some form of Yoga practice.

The actions of the yogi are truly benevolent because he is one who sees the Truth and is freed from all delusion, and also from the fear of death. How many like Nero intended to be good men, but found themselves rapidly fall into delusion and into fear when they were in a position of power! How many people can say that their good intentions have always led to the doing of real good? "Unless there is wisdom and freedom from fear," says great Confucius, "our benevolence is mere sentimentality." Until the Lord is known as one's own self in Samadhi, there is no freedom from fear and no real wisdom.

PRACTICAL PROGRAMME

Get up an hour earlier than usual, and determine to keep to this for six weeks, in order to give Yoga a fair trial. Wash the hands and feet on rising; stretch all over and then sit in the meditation posture (or as near as you can get) facing the East. Read some holy scripture for five minutes, slowly. Breathe deeply five times as in the section on Pranayama, and if you still feel restless count the breaths as previously explained. Relax the body, and mentally offer the meditation you are going to do to the Lord.

Now take a text for meditation and read it in a soft voice three times, then repeat it mentally three times more. "In Him the heaven, the earth, and the sky are woven, the mind also with all the senses. Know Him alone as the Self, and leave other thoughts." With patience support it in the mind, discarding without agitation interruptions from the senses or the mind itself. Remain calm in the meditation for ten minutes.

After the meditation, do the "line of light" practice given on page 44. Do this for another ten minutes.

At the end, repeat "OM" very slowly and softly 108 times. (Make 54 knots in a string, and use it as a rosary, going round it twice.) Do it with reverence, knowing that it is the highest name of truth and of God. It does not matter whether you fully understand this practice or not; it has been hallowed by the great yogis of many thousands of years and will produce its effect.

Finally, sit in the calm which these practices will bring, and give your friendliness and forgiveness to all. By this practice alone most nervous and emotional illnesses will be healed.

Return for another five minutes to the scripture with which you began.

During the day, make a break about midday and again in the evening, and in silence return to the thought of the meditation for a minute or more.

Whenever you have nothing to do, practise the "line of light."

In the evening, read one of the yogic texts for a quarter of an hour.

OBSTRUCTIONS

To the unconcentrated, life is one long series of interruptions and obstructions. They attribute the hindrance to outer objects. So beginners in Yoga tend to believe their circumstances peculiarly difficult.

A man asked the abbot of a monastery outside a city whether he could come each week-end to meditate there, as at home in the city there were constant hindrances and the noise from the street interrupted his meditation. "You may come," said the Abbot, "but there will still be interruptions." The man came the next week-end, and in the afternoon entered the great meditation hall, all alone. The place was absolutely silent, and quite bare except for a small image of the Bodhisattva of Wisdom at one end, with a single stick of incense burning in front of it. In the dim peace he felt his nerves relax and sat down to try to enter his meditation. After a little the place felt almost *too* silent; he thought he heard a tiny sound and opened his eyes a little. He noticed the stick of incense, and began to wonder why the smoke always rises. Then he noticed the perfume of the incense, far superior to the incense in the temple near his home. He speculated how much it might cost, and thought: "If it is not too expensive (and probably they get quite a reduction for buying in quantity) perhaps I could buy some from them here at cost price—they are after all spiritual men and not interested in profit —and then sell it to the priest at our temple and make a little for myself." The bell sounded, and he realized that his meditation hour was finished. He went straight to the Abbot, prostrated himself and said: "I understand. The interruptions are from within. From now on I shall practise meditation in my home. Please give me your blessing." The Abbot blessed him, and he returned.

While our desires and prayers and meditations relate to our individual selfish good, they have little result. But when our prayer becomes of the form: "O Lord, bless all and make me feel unity with all. Let me perform Thy will in the world, and do Thou, O Lord, appear within me and rule my soul," then the prayer is answered. When in the meditation the yogi begins to loose his clutch on the filthy blankets of egoity and selfishness in which he has wrapped himself, instead of holding them to him by his selfish desires, then cosmic forces begin to move, the karmas (path in life determined by one's own previous actions) adjust themselves rapidly, and the circumstances become more and more favourable to meditation. Holy Patanjali says that the world sometimes hinders and sometimes helps the ambitions and desires of the ordinary man, but in the case of the yogi, once he is making sincere efforts, all the forces of nature turn to help him. Everything that happens to the yogi, whatever it may seem to the people of the world, is a step on the stairway to Illumination. The yogi knows this, and even if illness and what others call disaster visit him, he does not become bewildered or demoralized by them. He recognizes in them the direct touch of the hand of the universal Lord.

COMMON SENSE IN TRAINING

Use common sense in Yoga, just as you would in any other

method of training. If you wanted to become a long-distance runner, it would be stupid to begin by trying to imitate a champion and run ten miles, because next day you would be collapsed and the muscles would be so stiff that you could not use them at all. You should run every single day without missing, but only so much as you can manage without strain. This doesn't mean, on the other hand, that you can have a day off because you feel a little tired or bored. That would defeat your object. In Yoga it is essential that you train every single day without fail, and you should also expect that occasionally you will get a feeling of boredom or impatience, just as a young student does at athletics or piano-playing or anything else. This feeling corresponds to the slight stiffening of the muscles, and the slight pain in them, that an athlete gets. If you understand it right, it is an encouraging sign; the pain in the muscles means that the muscles are growing and the body is adjusting to accommodate them. In the same way the mental "stiffness" means that the muscles of the will are developing.

THE PROCESS IN BRIEF

If a man has kept some items of the discipline, consciously or unconsciously, for some purpose or for no purpose, however it is, his mind will be invigorated and will begin to enquire deeper into the world's nature and his own nature. If he then consciously adopts the yogic discipline, his mind will be steady enough to take up meditation.

Through study of the authoritative writings of Yoga, he comes to know of the Reality which has been directly known by the great Yogis who have preceded him. By applying his reason and will to understand them, he comes to see that the theories underlying Yoga are not unreasonable. They are not yet proved, but he takes them as a working hypothesis. (Children hear that the world is revolving, but do not really believe it; when they study astronomy they see that it is not unreasonable to think it; later they can learn and perform certain experiments with pendulums by which they can directly perceive the rotation of the earth.)

In meditation the theories are confirmed. At the beginning

there are confirmations of small points only, but then it can seem reasonable that if we go on there will be confirmation of the rest also.

At first the world and the body in meditation are felt to be real, and the subject of meditation is only an idea. The "Reality beyond the mind" is just an assumption. As the meditation goes deeper, there are flashes of experience and then the subject of meditation becomes at least as real as the body. In the end of meditation the body and mind and the whole universe as now known to us are seen and known to be partly illusory—something superimposed on the Real as, in darkness, a snake is imagined where there was only a rope. Now the Lord, who had till then been fully manifest as Existence and partly manifest as Consciousness, becomes fully manifest as Consciousness also, so that the whole universe becomes alive to us, as it did to St. Francis. More, the Lord manifests Himself as Bliss, which had till then been hidden, and the universe turns into Bliss and Light.

FINAL HINTS

It is an advantage to join a spiritual group of traditional yogis, devoted solely to achieving Realization. The members of the group can do much to help each other over difficult places of the way.

It is an advantage to have a teacher, but it is not necessary to seek restlessly for one before beginning practice. If the practices are done with sincerity, the way to a true teacher will open. A true teacher never exploits his pupils economically, never imposes authority on them by bewildering them, is versed in the sacred scriptures and bases his teachings on passages in them, lives a life of sattva and has at least partially realized in his own experience what he teaches.

Those who want quick results should perform tapas in a spirit of great reverence for the Truth.

They are fortunate who can surrender all their actions and thoughts, successes and failures, desires and fears, and finally their whole ego, at the feet of the Lord.

4

THREE YOGIS

I. Rama Tirtha

SWAMI Rama Tirtha was a mathematician and scientist of modern India, who was also a fully illumined Mahatma. He was born in 1873 in the Punjab, of Gosain Brahmin parents. The family was poor but distinguished, and among his direct ancestors was Gosain Tulsidas, author of the Hindi *Ramayana*. The young Rama Tirtha had a brilliant academic career, specializing in mathematics, of which he finally became Professor at the University at Lahore.

Professor Rama Tirtha wrote for his pupils a pamphlet on how to excel in mathematics, based on his own practice. One of his rules was: "Try to do everything by your own unaided efforts; try as it were to re-discover everything". He recommended them, for instance, to read the enunciation of a geometrical proposition and then to try to work out their own demonstration of its proof. As a student he had practised this with such determination that he resolved to commit suicide if he ever failed. On one occasion he stayed up all night over one problem, and having to admit failure he actually prepared to take his own life. As he picked up the knife, he relates, he suddenly saw the solution as it were written in the air. "It was, of course, very wrong to decide to take my own life rather than ask for help from the teacher", adds Swami Rama, "but still it shows the spirit in which difficulties must be tackled and by which they are overcome". The story also shows two important sides to his character: independence and unbending will.

Yet there was something more in his character in favour of which he finally gave up the splendid career opening out before him. This was the desire to become a Mahatma. He came to see that the pursuit of truth through science was merely an offshoot of the impulse to know truth by direct experience He had been

religious from childhood, but religion did not give him immediate experience, and he determined to enter the traditional path
of Yoga. The process, however, required a Guru or spiritual
teacher. For a man of such acute intellect and independence of
mind it can have been no easy matter to accept a teacher. Nevertheless he found one, a Brahmin of average education but of
overwhelming spiritual attainments; from him the mathematician learnt the technique of transcending the finite mind.
The teacher was Shri Dada of Aligarh, whose biography is the
second of those given here.

Characteristically, Swami Rama focussed his whole will on the
meditation and other practices given him. One summer day he
set out from Rishikesha, where he was on holiday, and entered
Brahmapuri forest. His mind coloured in the deep dye of "I am
Shiva, I am Shiva" (I am the Supreme Reality) was but half
conscious of his physical surroundings. He resolved either to
have a direct perception of the Infinite Self or to end his physical
life in the endeavour. This was the Great Vow taken by Buddha
on the eve of Enlightenment, and it was foreshadowed in the
life of Swami Rama by his resolution either to master mathematics independently or give up his life. His shouts of OM
echoed and re-echoed in the valleys. He slept on the velvety
sands of the holy Ganges. Now oblivious to the outer environment, he climbed a high rock called Ganeshila which projects
far out into the water. Sitting on the rock he practised the
supreme affirmation: "I am Shiva, I am Shiva". The moon was
shining with all its brilliance and cloudlets dotted the sky. He
was at one with nature. He meditated on the verse of the Isha
Upanishad: "Where is there delusion, where grief, to him who is
established in Unity?" Suddenly he rose and walked to the edge
shouting: "I am Shiva, I am Shiva". He fell from that great height
into the deep water. His body sank far but it was brought to the
surface. When he opened his eyes there was one existence per-
vading all. Duality of matter and spirit had ended for ever. The
stars congratulated him; the mountains seemed to bow before
the great Knower who had passed into the realm beyond the
trio of knower, knowledge and known.

After his illumination his life became more and more that of a monk, and he felt drawn towards making a complete renunciation of the world. The ancient tradition is that the permission of a Guru must always be obtained before such a step. Although now fully illumined, Swami Rama followed the tradition and obtained the permission. Then he made provision for his wife and family, resigned from his position, and went up the Ganges route into the Himalayas of the state of Tehri. He lived as a wandering monk in the depths of the mountains, never touching money, begging his food or simply doing without it, on friendly terms with the numerous beasts of prey and other animals. To the villagers he seemed a god, impervious to hardship and fatigue, the friend of the spirits that dwelt in the rocks and trees. The photograph of Swami Rama on the front cover was taken soon after he had become a monk.

He had not left the world for ever. At the request of the Maharaja of Tehri he went to Japan to lecture on Vedanta and then to America. Many of the lectures were taken down and have been published under the title *In Woods of God-Realization*. After two years he returned and again went into the mountains, this time for good. But he continued to teach by his writings, the materials being brought to his cave by friends. His writings and lectures have made a deep and lasting impression on the hearts of many in India and elsewhere.

Swami Rama made no official disciples and founded no group. He now no longer saw individuals, but only the same Reality everywhere. In this period he wrote: "God must be at least as real as persons and things. To attach reality to the masks is to invite the wrath of the Reality which dwells behind them." His life had become simply the expression of his inner spiritual experience; impulses to write or speak came to him without conscious effort, as he says repeatedly. His realization was expressed both in the classical forms and also in terms of the scientific studies which had engaged his mind so long.

For instance, speaking of God seen in the Incarnations or in the spiritual teacher, he says that it is not that the weight of a body is actually concentrated at the centre of gravity (for that point is to all appearances like any other point), but for aught that concerns our mind, the mass is concentrated there. So God

is all-pervasive, immanent in nature, present equally everywhere;
yet in relation to our intellect, this universal Reality can be most
conveniently handled as if it were embodied in a personal being.
This personal being leads us from the visible to the Unseen.

He cites another analogy from mathematics to answer the
important question: Up to what point in spiritual progress is
there danger of relapse? The spiritual illumination can become
at last so high and strong as to be sovereign. Let us look upon
the human mind, he says, with its different possibilities of
equilibrium as a many-sided solid with different surfaces on which
it can lie flat. Then the mental revolution can be likened to the
spatial revolutions of such a body. Suppose that the spiritual
problem is to bring it from lying on surface A to lie on surface B.
As it is prised up, say by a lever, from the position in which it
lies on surface A, it will linger for a time unsteadily half-way up.
And if the lever now ceases to wedge it, it will tumble back or
relapse under the continuous pull of gravity. But if at last it
turns far enough for its centre of gravity to pass beyond surface
A altogether, the body will fall over on to surface B, and remain
there permanently. The pull of gravity towards A has vanished
and may now be disregarded. The polyhedron has become
immune against further attraction from that direction.

He answers with an arithmetical example the objection that
because Vedanta admits that Reality cannot be defined exactly, it
is therefore shadowy and vague. The relation between circum-
ference and diameter, he points out, cannot be exactly expressed
in arithmetical figures. But the relation itself is definite and
rational and is expressed by the Greek letter Pi. We can construct
it geometrically, and its actuality is observable in the mathe-
matical relations of the starry heavens, for the calculations of
which Pi is indispensable. Just so Reality, though not exactly
defined in words, is expressed by the word OM, and is known
as Existence-Consciousness-Bliss in deep meditation.

All knowledge, says Swami Rama in another of his notes, aims
at reaching the Unknown from the known, by dispelling Maya or
illusion. Knowledge must proceed from the starting point of
Self, which is the postulate and axiom of existence. Perfect knowledge is that whereby universal unity is established in the Self.

We verify it in a number of cases and finally see it in all concerns of life. In just the same way we verify the relation between the curve of the hyperbola and the asymptote up to a certain point, and for the rest we know for certain that the same relation subsists. So once the Self is known as the substratum of the universe, there are no further questions about it which need be answered.

Swami Rama carried his views to their logical conclusion. Reality must be known in the arms of the bear, in the tiger's mouth. We must see the Reality of God alone acting through all things, their seeming forms being non-entity. Similarly causality must be replaced by the vision of God. Compare the view of causation taken by the primitive, by the educated and by the illumined. To the first, superstitious and credulous, almost anything might be a causal agent. To the more advanced, many of these supposed causes are unreal, have no force. The true seer feels no force at all in anything but God; to him no suggested causes have any reality. The question now arises, if we give up all regard to causation, if we see in the different objects God and God alone, how shall we undertake action, how will the body be preserved? Swami Rama gives the same answer that Christ gave, the answer of the Avadhut or total renunciate: "As a faithful wife, when loved, attends cheerfully to all the household duties of her own accord, but when we seem to love another, she is stricken with jealousy and the household affairs are all neglected —so God attends to all we need if we love nothing but the Supreme". And again: "Not until you have given up the seeming objects will you see the infinite faithfulness and love which is in the things of this world; not till you have laid aside the garb of names and forms can you see the God hidden therein". As to action: "While in God, the right methods, the right impulses, the right inspiration, the right inclinations spontaneously well up in the heart and lead us. The fully illumined man lacks the ordinary springs of motive and cannot be influenced by profit and loss, counsel of friends, unexpected news and so on. But in him the right acts become as spontaneously imperative as the demands of a healthy appetite. And to him, to perform the right acts brings as much immediate satisfaction as the satisfaction of the appetite brings to ordinary men".

Many times and with many illustrations Swami Rama repeats the central point of his teaching. "You look out from the high window on the things in the street, but if you try to get them directly by jumping from the window you will be smashed to pieces. You have to go down and come out of the front door. So you may see the things of the world, but to enjoy them truly you must turn away from them, go within and pass through the door of Illumination. To try to enjoy them directly leads to disaster." "Correct yourself first and all else will be corrected or become corrigible. Never otherwise. Let the order for correction to the environments go through the right channel, and with the seal of the magistrate upon it—the seal of Illumination. Anything that the magistrate tries to carry out personally, and not as the order of the Bench, will cause only violent resistance. But any constable, with the uniform on, can arrest even the greatest in the land".

All the events of the world, concludes Swami Rama, are to be seen not as chains of cause and effect, but as servants of God who is the highest Self. Their purpose is to drive man to Godhead. All the great tragedies, the illnesses, the sufferings physical and mental, have only this object. The King has gone out incognito into the city, and sees something in a private house which he wants. He tries to seize it directly, and the police come and arrest him without recognizing him. But when he returns to the palace with them and resists no more, he is recognized and sits on the throne and is obeyed by them. Just so Swami Rama looked upon physical illness and all other events. "They whip me and stab me when I enter this hovel of body-consciousness; but they obey me when I occupy the Throne of Illumination".

Towards the end of his short life of thirty-three years, Swami Rama swam every day in the strong mountain river, in spite of his weakness. One day he was caught in a whirlpool and carried away. The thing was seen by a hillman who could not swim. He said that Swami Rama made three attempts to get out of the current, and failing, cried strongly and clearly: "If it is to go, then let it go! Om, Om, Om!" Then he was carried away.

It was clear from a note found among his papers that he expected to leave the body soon. The body had become useless and almost unknown to him, who had become the One of whom the Upanishad says: "From fear of him, fire burns; from fear of him, the sun shines; from fear of him, the deities carry out their duties; from fear of him, Death moves on his way".

II. Shri Dada

Narayana Prasad, later known as Shri Dada, was born in a rich family in Aligarh, a city of the United Provinces, in 1858. He was a Brahmin, or member of the highest caste. In early youth he met his Guru, Swami Krishnanandaji, and devoted himself entirely to his service. The young man's father strongly disapproved, because he wished his son to live the life of an aristocrat; in the end he disinherited him and refused to see him again. Shri Dada would not take his worldly troubles to his Guru and spent some months penniless, living in the woods. Later he got a post as a clerk at the railway station and in this way supported himself, remaining in the service for the rest of his life. He gave himself with undivided will to the personal service of his Guru and to the mystic practices he was taught, and he obtained the final illumination when still quite young.

He was now a Mahatma, but remained a householder, supporting his wife and family and founding groups of disciples in the towns to which his work took him.

He was not a great theorist of Yoga—he did not know classical Sanskrit; but he was an expert on the practice. Of course he had a good knowledge of the philosophical basis, and his knowledge had been completely verified in his own experience. He was like one who had learnt a language by residence in the country rather than from grammars. So it was that he did not become famous as a Pandit or philosopher. The great abbots of the ancient monasteries founded by Shankaracharya knew him as a Mahatma; his disciples knew him as a Guru; but the general public simply knew him as a very saintly man.

Nevertheless, his influence was considerable. He made the first move towards removing the prejudice against the "Untouchables", a move which could only be made effectively by a Brahmin, one of the highest caste. The removal of the disabilities attached to the Untouchables later became the life-work of Mahatma Gandhi, but it must be remembered that the latter was only a member of the Vaishya or merchant caste, and the reform would never have been accepted in practice if it had not originally come from the Brahmin caste. Shri Dada was regarded by some as a traitor to his caste and was abused and even physically attacked for his convictions. Some of his bitterest opponents later became his disciples.

In the same spirit he broke with the custom that the religious instruction of the Upanishads should not be given to women. It was not that he did not believe in tradition—he had the greatest veneration for it—but he attacked meaningless prejudices based on one-sided interpretation of a few doubtful texts, and quoted the lives of the great Incarnations, who had women and Untouchables among their closest disciples and friends. On one occasion when the rumour went round that he was initiating two women disciples, a mob stormed the house. The Mahatma confronted them and was able at once to turn them to his own view.

He was a universal saint, with no prejudice or bias against anyone. He studied the Koran and entertained the Moslem mystics in his own home. Similarly he made his disciples read the Gospels and revere the teachings of Christ as a perfect revelation of truth. The great teacher often said that the association of India and Britain would be an important factor in the spiritual history of the world; he believed that Britain had much to teach India, and had no sympathy with those who wished to break the association by violent means. But he also thought that Britain must learn from India the philosophy and practice of Yoga.

He did not recommend his disciples to retire from the world, but told them to make a success of their lives, physically, mentally and spiritually. The only point of having a healthy body, economic independence, a developed mind, was to realize God in the Self. When God was known in the Self, there was an experience of unending bliss, which no worldly catastrophe could shake; until God was known, life was suffering. He asked intellectual people to study history to find whether worldly success alone had ever brought lasting happiness to anyone. With simple people, he appealed to their own experience of life;

insecurity was itself a cause of suffering, and what was secure in life? When it was fully understood that the changing objects of the world could not give lasting satisfaction, their irrational attraction would cease. Taking an illustration familiar to the common people, he pointed out that a child is attracted by the bright colour of an unripe mango and goes to eat it. But when, after repeated disappointments, he understands that mangoes of that colour are not good to eat, the colour no longer attracts him.

Those disciples who were philosophically inclined were told to analyse the occasions when they thought they had experienced real bliss. He showed them that in such cases the sense of the individual separate "I" was temporarily absent. The technique of Yoga was to purify and still the mind, and in that state to dissolve the sense of egoity, which is illusory, in God, the true Self.

By many illustrations, by lucid and profound argument, he convinced many disciples of the theoretical principles of Yoga, and some of them by giving their whole energies to the practice attained the realization that ends suffering.

For people living in the world he specially recommended meditation on incidents in the lives of Incarnations or of great saints, and also the ancient practice, which Kobo Daishi made the basis of his own system, of repeating one of the great Names of God: Rama, Jesus or OM.

After a long illness, during which he continued and even intensified his teachings, Shri Dada died at Hapur in 1910.

III. Kobo Daishi

Kobo Daishi was born in A.D. 774 as the son of the governor of Sanuki province of Japan. He went to the university at the capital to master Chinese classics and poetry, Confucianism, Taoism and Buddhism. At twenty he became a monk, and at twenty-four, when sitting in meditation on a cliff by the seashore, there was an experience of illumination which determined his life. His learning and piety so impressed the Emperor that he commissioned Kobo to go to China to find the inner heart of Buddhism and bring the knowledge back to Japan. Buddhism, of course, was already established in Japan, but for two centuries it had developed mostly within a small circle on Hinayana lines, without any extensive appeal.

Kobo studied under various masters in China, including Indian teachers from Kashmir and Southern India, from whom he learned Sanskrit. Finally, at the capital Chang-An he met a very old teacher, the patriarch of the Mantrayana or sect of the True Word. When Kobo arrived, this master said: "I have been awaiting you so long. Now at last you have come". He told him to make ready quickly to receive the teachings, and in a few months Kobo was made his successor in the patriarchal line. The master said: "Now go back quickly to your own country, present the doctrine to the Emperor, then spread it among your people and so promote their welfare". After this charge, the master died in a few days. Kobo's ship was caught in a typhoon on the way home, and it took fifty-five days to accomplish the journey to Japan, which today takes only twenty-four hours. He found that his patron the Emperor Kammu had died, but he presented to the new Emperor many sutras, pictures and relics from China, and then left the court for over a year, devoting himself to arranging and studying the material he had brought, to travelling as a begging monk, and to his yogic practices.

Three years later, again a new Emperor ascended the throne. This was the brilliant Emperor Saga, a poet and painter of distinction, and—perhaps an even higher accomplishment—a great calligrapher. He was one of the so-called "Three Great Calligraphers" of the period, the others being Hayanari Tachibana and Kobo Daishi. As a natural result, they became intimate friends, and the Emperor granted great favours to Kobo. From this Emperor the saint received as a gift, Mt. Koya, on which he built a monastery which today is probably the largest in Japan. From this time on the sect of the True Word or Mantra was established on a firm foundation.

It is hard even to list the secular achievements of the versatile genius of Kobo Daishi. In scholarship, painting and calligraphy he was not merely among the best of his time, but of the whole of the cultural history of the Far East. Where we should say "even Homer nods", the standard Japanese proverb is "even Kobo makes a mistake". He introduced tea into Japan, invented

This picture, by a Japanese Zen abbot, is a representation of illumination. The monk having climbed the hill of meditation is at rest in Samadhi, and Truth (symbolised as the peerless Mount Fuji) reveals itself to him above the mists of duality.

a new writing brush, built reservoirs for irrigation, constructed bridges, and set up public baths at medicinal hot-springs, some of which he himself discovered.

In his time education was not open to the children of families below the fifth rank; in other words, the common people were completely shut out. Kobo opened near the capital the "Institution of Liberal Arts and Wisdom" for the children of the commoners. The education given was of two kinds, secular and sacred. The secular students were taught Confucianism (note the tolerance of this Buddhist priest), Chinese composition and writing, grammar and the principles of ethics. Those who wished to become priests could choose to study the True Word teachings or those of any other sect, and in addition were required to master a good deal of secular learning.

The best epitome of Kobo Daishi's gifts is the invention of the Japanese alphabet. Before his time the language had no alphabet of its own and had to be written by using random Chinese characters having approximately the same phonetic value as the syllables to be written—a clumsy system indeed. Perhaps Kobo's Sanskrit studies convinced him of the advantages of a phonetic script—at any rate, it was he who first classified the fifty syllables of the language in the most scientific way (still used in the grammars) following the Sanskrit model, and selected certain simplified symbols to represent them. So far the scholar. Then the poet in him thought that for teaching the new alphabet he would embody the syllables in a poem in a particular metre, using each syllable once and once only. But Kobo was not only scholar and poet, he was also a saint. He decided that his poem should declare the essence of Buddhism, and chose four lines of the Nirvana-sutra as representing the heart of the Buddhist doctrine, to paraphrase in his poem. The stanza in the original Sutra is as follows:

"All earthly things pass away:
 This is the law of all existence.
 Going beyond this law of extinction,
 We are in the bliss of Nirvana alone".

The extreme difficulty of the task may be imagined, but Kobo solved it brilliantly with a poem of great beauty:

"The blooms are fragrant, but alas! they fall.
Who in this world can remain for ever?
Crossing this day the mountains of transient existence
We see no more shallow dreams, nor are deluded".

In this poem, each letter of the Japanese alphabet occurs in the original once and only once. For over a thousand years, it has been repeated by every Japanese who recites the alphabet, or uses a dictionary. There is still in existence a manuscript with the poem brushed by Kobo in his wonderful calligraphy, in the new symbols selected by him—the whole representing one of the most remarkable feats of secular and religious genius in history.

Kobo's achievements in the spiritual realm are no less impressive. He wrote a great many works, most of them still extant, developing and expounding his system. He always stressed the fact that man can realize his Buddha nature in this very life, and it is not to be sought for in the state after death.

His life and teachings show certain salient points, which include the following: Deep learning, Unity, Joy, Benevolence and Humility, and Illumination.

Of his deep learning enough has been said, but it is noteworthy that he never condemned other systems of thought, whether Buddhist or even outside Buddhism. As has been seen, he did not expect everyone to master the complete Buddhist doctrine, and at his university, Confucianism and other branches of secular learning were taught. It was partly this broad tolerance which enabled him to found his sect with so little opposition.

Unity is a fundamental doctrine in his system. All beings, living and even inert, have as their essence the nature of Buddha, which, however, transcends them. In fact it is only the Buddha-nature which has absolute reality. From the point of view of meditation technique, certain objects such as the sun, are more easily taken as symbols of the essential Buddha-nature than others. By prolonged concentration on such a symbol, the mind easily becomes completely one-pointed, and then the symbolized is seen in the symbol. In the same way, the mantras or certain mystic syllables are meditated upon to focus the mind. It is hinted that the meditation on the mantras can also give great powers, but in the teaching of Kobo the aim is illumination. Meditation on a mantra, such as the word OM, or the syllables A-BI-RA-UN-GEN, with concentration on the sound and on the meaning, is said by Kobo to be one of the most direct ways to illumination, and for this reason the sect is known as the Sect of the True Word or Mantra. It is, in fact, the doctrine of mantra as taught in the classical yoga of India. As further aids to concentration, mystic diagrams are used and certain gestures with the hands. All these things have deep spiritual meaning, but the purpose is simply to bring serenity and concentration to the mind so that it may realize the Buddha-nature in itself and in everything.

The illumination brings with it Joy, which expresses itself in realization of beauty in conduct, in thought and in art. Kobo's whole life was a work of art, and it might be said that the productions of his hands almost founded Japanese culture. Some account of his significance in the history of Far Eastern art is given in Fenollosa's *Epochs of Chinese and Japanese Art*.

Of his universal benevolence enough has been said, but it might perhaps be thought that such a man would have every reason to be proud of his fame. It is sufficient to say that this teacher, the most learned and gifted man of the age, often travelled for long periods as an angya or mendicant monk in remote parts of the country where he was not recognized. There is a life-sized bronze statue of the master as an angya, his thick powerful body clad in a shabby robe, carrying only a staff, begging-bowl and rosary, and on the massive head a big round straw hat throwing the face into shadow. In this way the great genius elected to pass years of his life.

The glory of his illumination was experienced even by those who might have felt their interests threatened by his activities. After the foundation of the True Word in Japan, a great meeting of all the Buddhist sects was held at the Imperial Court, and in long debates Kobo established his doctrine against the objections of the other sects. The accounts say that he entered into meditation during the discussions and that all saw a brilliant radiance coming from his body. It is certain that the others were not antagonised by the triumph of the new sect, and good relations prevailed during the rest of Kobo's life.

In his sixty-second year, he entered the final meditation, entrusting future affairs to his disciples with detailed instructions. The tradition is that he did not die but passed into a trance, and is concealed somewhere in the dense and mysterious forests of Mount Koya. When the next Buddha incarnates, Kobo will emerge to greet him.

As has been seen, a characteristic doctrine of the teacher is that of mantra. The use of mantra is, however, not confined to the True Word sect nor to Buddhism, but has been well-known to nearly all great mystics. Here are two quotations on mantra from the other two Mahatmas whose lives have been briefly described in this chapter:—

Swami Rama Tirtha: "All the planes of being, all the worlds, all phases of existence are covered by the syllable OM. When chanted it puts the mind in a state where it is one with God. This is a fact which can be verified by experience".

Shri Dadaji: "From the Yogic point of view, all spiritual learning is contained in one word, and it is OM. If you want any worldly advantage such as wealth, health or power, then you may concentrate on other words such as Rama or Hari, but if you want to see God within your soul then OM is the best object of your concentration".

In conclusion here is an extract from one of the works of Kobo Daishi, the *Jewel Key*. The translation is that of Dr. Anezaki:—

"Vast, vast, extremely vast
Are the scrolls of yellow silk,
Hundreds and thousands of the Inner teachings and the
  Outer.
Profound, profound, very profound
Ways are marked and ways shown, hundreds of ways.
What benefit in writing and reading, finally to die?
Unknown and unknowable, self never knows self;
Thinking, thinking and thinking, yet no signs of wisdom!
Mad are the beings in the three realms of existence

And none knowing his own madness;
Blind are the beings, born of the egg or the womb,
And yet all unaware of their blindness!
Born, born and reborn without limit,
And still dark as to the origin of birth;
Dying, dying, and dying without end,
Yet veiled is the ultimate goal of life.
The healing power of the Outer doctrines has wiped away
    all dust;
Now opens the store of the True Word,
By which the hidden treasures are brought to light,
In which are embodied all virtues and power.
The Buddhas in the innumerable Buddha-lands
Are nothing but the Buddha within our own soul;
The Golden Lotus, multitudinous as the drops of ocean
    water,
Is living in our own body.
Myriads of figures are contained in every mystic letter;
Every piece of matter embodies a Deity.
On realizing this, every one shall attain
The glory of Illumination in this very life".

5

ILLUSTRATIVE PASSAGES FROM THE LITERATURE OF YOGA

The following translations of prayers ·from the Vedas are based on the celebrated commentary of Sayanacharya and the gloss of Swami Dayananda Saraswati.

I.

O Self-illumined Lord, Thou hast created all effulgent objects such as the sun, moon and stars! Thou art the only Master of the Universe! O Consciousness supreme, Thou wert the one Lord and one Existence before creation. Now Thou dost give support to Thy creations—the suns and the planets. Grant that we may ever engage in the practices of Yoga to please Thee, and may we ever be devoted to Thee!

(Yajur Veda)

II.

He who supports within Himself the heavenly bodies, the earth and all that it contains; He who is the embodiment of happiness and release, free from all pain; He who protects all; He who controls the movement of the atoms and of the solar systems; may we, with devotion and purpose, offer adoration to that most desirable One, that we may attain to union with Him.

(Rig Veda)

III.

Ye men! Let us unite to offer perpetual devotion to the Lord, Who is our Brother, the Creator of the Universe, the Fulfiller of all our desires, Who knows the whole universe and also our births. The learned Yogis, having attained the state of conscious immortality, abide in Him who is free from all suffering, and

77

Who is Bliss Absolute. That Lord is our Guru (Teacher), our Sovereign, and the source of justice.

(Yajur Veda)

IV.

The learned who are engaged in the good of others night and day, whose souls are decorated with divine knowledge, attain immortality and release. These travellers in the realm of perpetual light, who are without sin, and whose minds have been universalised, these illumined ones keep their bodies for the enlightenment of others.

(Yajur Veda)

V.

May my mind ever think of the good of all beings!
That mind which is a means of divine knowledge, which takes man far, far during the waking state, which causes objects to be known to the senses, which abides in the subtle cause in the state of sleep—
May that mind ever think of the good of all beings!

The mind which manifests its modifications in the form of the intellect, will and memory, which is the means of accomplishing the good of all people, may that mind be directed towards justice and the exercise of truth and love—
And may it ever think of the good of all beings!

The mind which, when engaged in the practice of Yoga and devotion, acquires a knowledge of the past, future and present, through which the laws of the world are known—
May that mind ever think of the good of all beings!

The mind in which a knowledge of the four Vedas abides in seed form, which has the capacity to know what is best for all beings—
May that mind of mine ever think of the good of all beings!

The mind which controls and leads the senses as a charioteer directs his horses, the mind abiding in the region of the heart,

which never grows old and whose speed is inconceivable—
May that mind of mine ever think of the good of all beings!

(Yajur Veda)

VI.

Grant, O Lord, that I may have no fear of my friends or of my
enemies or of any object known or unknown! Grant that I may
pass my nights and days without fear! May the four directions
and all who dwell in them be my friends!

(Sama Veda)

THE UPANISHADS

In the Katha Upanishad, the child Nachiketas is instructed by
the God Yama in the secret of immortality.

Yama said:
"The pleasant is different from the highest good. Each serves a
different end. Those who choose the highest good come to
eternal happiness. Those who care for what is pleasant to the
senses or to the lower strata of the intellect do not come to the
true end.

"O child, you have given up all longing for earthly things and
objects of beautiful form which people generally desire. Indeed,
you know their real value. Nor have you cared for physical riches
which are the deep waters in which many thoughtless people
sink.

"There are two mutually exclusive paths, each leading to a
different goal. They are the path of ignorance and the path of
knowledge. My son, you ask for the knowledge of Truth, and
you are fit for it because the host of earthly desires has not
moved your soul.

"There are men who have their home in the world (sansara),
that is, in the midst of darkness and ignorance. They consider
themselves to be wise, clever and learned. They stumble along
the zig-zag path of the world like the blind led by the blind

"The foolish man has no idea of the future. He is blinded by ignorance and loves wealth. He thinks 'this world belongs to me and I do not need anything else'. Such a man is born and dies again and again, and his life is a perpetual dark well of suffering.

"Logic and reasoning, however subtle, do not lead one to the realization of the infinite and blissful Self. One must be taught by another who knows the truth.

"Wealth, fame and other mundane advantages are all uncertain. How can the Immutable be obtained by the changing? Perishable things are to be offered as oblations in the fire of devotion-wisdom; thus is the Eternal, the Imperishable attained.

"O dear child, blessed are you that your heart is fixed on the goal of all desires, the one support of the whole universe temporal and psychological, the one eternal fruit of devotion, the region of fearlessness, the one really praiseworthy state which is majestic and infinite. You have courageously rejected all that is opposed to it.

"The man of keen intelligence restrains his mind from the objective world and focusses it on his true Self (Atman) which is most ancient, hard to perceive, and abides secretly in the innermost cave of the intellect. He transcends joy and grief by realising this Atman, which appears to be seated in the dark surroundings of the mind.

"The goal of all wisdom and scriptural learning extolled by the Vedas, which is attainable by austerity, charity, renunciation and so forth, and desiring which men lead the life of Brahma-charya—that goal, epitomized in one word, is OM.

"This word is verily Brahman. It is the highest. He who knows its meaning and worships it attains the goal he seeks.

"The Self (Atman) is not born, nor does it ever die. It does not come from anywhere, nor can it be pointed to as anything in the objective world. It is unborn, eternal, everlasting and most ancient. It survives the death of the body.

"This Atman is more minute than the minutest. It is greater than the great. It abides in the heart of every living being. He who is free from desire and whose senses and mind rest in undisturbable serenity can see the majesty of Atman and is no longer subject to worry or grief".

The following verses concerning Brahman (the supreme Reality) are translated from the Svetasvatara Upanishad:

"Brahman supports the universe which is a combination of the manifest and the unmanifest, the perishable and the imperishable. The individual soul is not the Ruler as it is limited by the self-imposed conditions of an enjoyer. It is freed from all limitations when it knows the nature of the supreme Ruler.

"By knowing the self-shining One, all the limitations of ignorance end for ever. With the cessation of all sufferings, there is release from birth and death. He who meditates on Him as Virat, the sole cause of the universe, on the death of the body finds identity with the Lord of the universe. By meditating upon Brahman, and transcending every relation with the world, a person becomes Brahman.

"This Brahman should be meditated upon as eternal, as dwelling in one's own soul as its essence. Besides Brahman there is nothing else to be known. It is the enjoyer (the individual soul), the object of enjoyment and the arbiter of the destiny of all beings (Ishvara). He who knows Brahman in these three forms achieves liberation.

"It is by pressing the sesamum seed that its oil is extracted. It is by churning milk curds that butter is formed. It is by digging a well that subterranean water can be induced to gush forth. It is by rubbing two pieces of wood together that fire is drawn out of them. Similarly Brahman, the Absolute Self, is cognized within one's own soul by practising a life of truth and self-discipline (tapas).

5

"The wise man holds his body steady with the upper part (the chest, neck and head) kept in line. The senses are withdrawn and the mind subdued. Then he meditates on Savitri. This is the raft called OM upon which all the dangerous currents of the world are crossed.

"Before full concentration on Brahman is effected, the yogi in his meditation sees Brahman in the form of frost, smoke, sun, wind, fire, fire-flies, lightning, crystal and the moon.
(*Note*: Before the mind is fully absorbed in Brahman it sees the forms mentioned in this verse, which mark the stages by which the mind is raised to the Brahman-consciousness. This is not an universal and essential experience of every yogi; these manifestations may or may not occur).

"When the yogi is absorbed in full concentration, he sees in his own self, like a light, the true nature of Brahman, who is eternal and free from all changes and modifications. Then he goes beyond the effects of ignorance and, having known Brahman as his Self, is released from all bonds".

THE BHAGAVAD GITA

In Chapter VI of the Bhagavad Gita, the Lord Krishna speaks to his pupil Prince Arjuna about Yoga:

"When a man, renouncing all desires, ceases to regard himself as the doer in respect of actions and the pursuit of sense-objects, he is said to be rooted in Yoga.
"A man must raise himself by his own efforts, and must not allow himself to be dragged down. He alone is his own friend, and he alone is his own enemy.
"To the man who has conquered his mind by the self, his self is verily a friend; but to him who is not the master of the kingdom of his mind and senses, his self is like an enemy.
"The devotee who has conquered his mind, body and senses, who has acquired perfect serenity, whose finite self has recognized the supreme Self to be his Self—he is undisturbed by heat and cold, pleasure and pain, honour and dishonour.
"That Yogi who has found supreme satisfaction in the theoretical

knowledge of the Self, and who has in actual intuitive experience realised that knowledge, who is master of his senses—he is called a true Yogi, and to him a lump of earth, a stone and gold are the same.

"He is foremost among those who have attained to success in Yoga who extends equal love to the righteous, the unrighteous, friend, foe, those who are neutral, kinsmen, saint and sinner.

"Rooted in wisdom, living in solitude, his mind and body under control, hoping for nothing, possessing nothing, the Yogi must at all times try to keep his mind tranquil.

"Seated in a pure place, established in a firm posture on a seat which should be neither too high nor too low and composed of a cloth covering a skin which is laid upon a base of kusha grass, concentrating the mind on one object, mastering the motion of the mind and senses, he should practise the Yoga which leads to the purification of the mind.

"With his body, neck and head erect, firm and unmoving, let him look steadfastly at the tip of his nose.

"Let him make his mind tranquil, practising the vow of continence (brahmacharya), fixing his controlled mind on Me. Let him make Me his supreme goal.

"The Yogi who thus masters his mind is in the end ever united with Me. He goes to the supreme spiritual peace which is found only in Me.

"He who eats too much or who abstains from food cannot be a Yogi, nor can he who is given to too much sleep, nor can he who is always wakeful, O Arjuna.

"Yoga destroys the sufferings of the one who eats moderately and enjoys life moderately, whose efforts are balanced and who is moderate in his sleeping and waking.

"When his thought, perfectly controlled, is centred on the Self alone, free from longings for sense-objects, he is called a saint.

"As a lamp in a sheltered place flickers not, even so is the controlled mind of the Yogi who practises concentration on the Self.

"When, through the practice of meditation, the mind has been tranquillized and subjugated, then the Yogi sees the supreme Self in his individual self and is satisfied.

"When through his intuitive faculty (buddhi) the wise man has experienced that extreme joy which surpasses all sense experience, when steadfast in the contemplation of his higher Self he never moves from the reality, when he experiences transcendental delight which he holds higher than any other acquisition and, being rooted in it, not even great pain can move him—this is called Yoga, this parting for ever from suffering. One must practise this Yoga with unwavering will and a heart not susceptible to despondency.

"Giving up entirely and for ever all clinging desires born of ambition or imagination, let him restrain his senses from going in all directions by using discrimination.

"Slowly and firmly, steadying the intellect (buddhi), let him withdraw his mind from the world; then, uniting it by meditation with the Self, let him not think of anything else.

"When the wavering mind, as yet unsteady, wanders away, let him again restrain it and fix it upon the Self.

"The Yogi who has tranquillized his mind and subdued his passions, who is free from the taint of ignorance (avidya), becomes one who is liberated in life (jivanmukta).

"That enlightened yogi, his mind fixed in meditation, easily obtains union (yoga) with the supreme Spirit and, being without sin, enjoys infinite bliss.

"That yogi whose self is matured in Yoga, who sees all beings abiding in his Self and his Self as the essence of all beings, loves all beings equally.

"He who sees Me in everything and the whole universe in Me—I am ever present to him as he is ever mindful of Me.

"He who worships Me, realising the identity of his Self with Me who am the substance of all beings—that Yogi, whatever his mode of life, verily abides in Me.

"He who regards all beings as his own Self and treats them with the same consideration as he would show himself, whether he is confronted with pleasure or pain—he is a great Yogi."

YOGA VASISHTHA

In the Yoga Vasishtha, the sage Vasishtha instructs his pupil Rama in the following words:

"This world is composed of reality and unreality, and bears the stamp of the Almighty; it is made up of unity and duality and is yet free from either.

"The perverted intellect which considers itself as the body, is verily confined in it; but when it knows itself to be identical with the taintless Self (Atman), it is liberated from its confinement.

"Brahman is all in all; He is perfect peace, secondless, without equal or comparison. He expands Himself by His own power as the Infinite, and stretches His mind in three different directions—creation, preservation and dissolution.

"The mind being curbed, with its senses and organs centred in the Self (Atman), there appears a dazzling light before it and the unreal world fades away, as the shades of night disappear before the light of the sun.

"The imaginary world recedes from view and falls like a withered leaf, and the soul (jiva) remains like a fired grain, without the power of vegetation or reproduction.

"The intellect, cleared of the cloud of illusion which overhung the deluded mind, shines as clearly as the vault of the autumnal sky.

"I have now told you, O Rama-ji, of the curbing and weakening of the mind, which is the first step towards the beatification of the soul by Yoga. Now I will tell you about the second step, the edification and strengthening of the intellect.

"With boundless patience, courage and service, carry on your meditations and self-study, and worship God in the holy Yoga. Remember, a miserly soul, a greedy soul, a soul believing in its superiority over others, will not see God.

"By continued perseverance in this course, the pilgrim is led a great distance on the way, to a state which transcends all my powers of description, but which may be felt by the devotee as he advances on his path. All is goodness and peace when in this yogic state. The syllable OM is the symbol of the whole.

"Hear now the method of the worship of God, O my beloved pupil. In all forms of worship you must cease to think of your body, and separate your mind from your personality. You must then apply your mind diligently, under the guidance of your Teacher, to thinking of the pure and bodiless Spirit, which witnesses the operations of the body from within.

"True worship consists in inward meditation alone, and in no outer form of worship; therefore, apply your mind to the adoration of the universal Spirit by meditating within yourself.

"He is the form of the intellect, the source of all light, and glorious as millions of suns! He is the inner light of the mind. His head and shoulders reach above the heaven of heavens; His lotus-like feet descend far below the lowest abyss of space.

"The worlds rolling over one another rest on a corner of His capacious bosom. His effulgence passes beyond the limits of the unlimited void. Above, below, in all four quarters and on all sides of the compass He extends, undiminished and without end.

"He encompasses within Himself this mundane sphere and all other worlds, their mountains and all they contain; and all-powerful Time, which hurls them ever onward, is the warder at the threshold of His eternity.

"He is seated in the midst of all things, and is the sole giver of strength and energy to all. That thou art! (Tat tvam asi!)

"O, adore Him in yourself! He requires no illumination or burning of incense.

"By constantly talking of this holy subject and continually returning to this enquiry when it has been broken off, one becomes fully conscious of the Self."

THE ASHTAVAKRA GITA

The word *Gita* means a song. The translator found this Gita, a few verses of which are reproduced here, a favourite text among the Mahatmas of the Himalayan regions. Each verse is a text for meditation:

"The nature of the Self is absolute, immutable, taintless. It is not distant, nor is it subject to attainment. This is Truth.

"In those who have cognized the Self, illusion is dispelled, and the light of pure consciousness shines through them. Their distress is at an end and they live in bliss.

"The wise know that all that is not the Self is merely a movement of the mind; being liberated, they live as a child lives.

"All such ideas as 'this am I' and 'this I am not' end in the conviction that all is the Self. Realizing this, the yogi becomes silent.

"For the yogi who has become inwardly calm, there is no distraction and no concentration, no increase or decrease of knowledge, no joy and no grief.

"The dominion of Heaven or indigence, profit or loss, society or solitude, are the same to the yogi who has realized his nature to be free from all conditions.

"The yogi who is liberated while yet in life has no further duties to perform, nor is his heart attached to anything. His actions in this world are appearances only.

"The yogi who has passed beyond the region of desires, finds no significance in phenomena, in the universe, in contemplation on That, or in liberation.

"He who sees reality in the universe may try to negate it. Not so the Mahatma who has rooted out all desires; not seeing, he appears to see.

"He who is conscious of distraction, practises self-control; the illumined sage, having nothing further to accomplish, has no need of self-discipline.

"Though the man of spiritual knowledge appears to act like others, in fact he does not do so, for he sees no necessity for samadhi, nor does he perceive distraction or any taint in his own essence.

"Free from desire, he is neither conscious of existence nor of non-existence, but is ever satisfied and wise; though appearing to act, nothing is done by him in reality.

"He who experiences the supreme bliss of his own nature and whose mind is ever tranquil and pure, he has no need to renounce, nor does he feel the lack of anything in himself.

"The mind of the sage does not give rise to the modifications of concentration, distraction or prejudice; his actions are not subject to any code, nor is he affected by honour or dishonour.

"He who still retains his egoism is mentally active even when at rest; but the wise man who is free from egoism is incapable of sin or wrong action.

"The mind of the sage is free from effort whether meditating or acting. His actions and meditations are not prompted by personal motives.

"Whether he lives a life of action or withdraws from the world, the ignorant man does not find spiritual peace, whereas the sage discovers the truth and so becomes happy for ever".

POEM BY SWAMI RAMA TIRTHA

This poem translated from the Urdu is a fine example of Swami Rama Tirtha's style of writing:

"O silvery peak of the Himalayas,
Thou art the mother of the divine science.
May thy lap ever be full;
May Girija ever play in thy arms.
Give the monsoons the divine message—
When they rain in the plains they must impregnate the corn
With the great truth 'I am God'.
May he who tastes the fruits be intoxicated with unity.
May he involuntarily proclaim
Without the least doubt
The cry rising from the height of Mount Kailash:
'Om Tat Sat! Om Tat Sat! Om!'

Visit the assembly of roses, O breeze,
And the hearts of the brave.
To the ears of those who are startled by thy soft touch
Sweetly convey the great secret,
Without the least doubt,
The cry rising from the height of Mount Kailash:
'Om Tat Sat! Om Tat Sat! Om!'

Flash, O lightning, on the world.
Fill with light our dark homes.
Quicken and illumine all hearts;
Crush their doubts for evermore.
From the height of Mount Kailash rises the cry:
'Om Tat Sat! Om Tat Sat! Om!'

O lightning, flash brightly. O thunder, crash
And annihilate all duality, prejudice and illusion.
Let them hear the mighty cry
And abandon all doubts, all scepticism.

From the height of Mount Kailash rises the cry:
'Om Tat Sat! Om Tat Sat! Om!'

Flow on and on, O Mother Ganges,
Mayst thou be a source of peace to the world
For long, long ages. Impregnate with the great truth
Every atom of the body of those who drink thy water.
Kill all their doubts and scepticism.
From the height of Mount Kailash rises the cry:
'Om Tat Sat! Om Tat Sat! Om!'

Ye editors, in the columns of your journals
Publish the cry from Mount Kailash in letters bold.
Ye instructors, in your schools
Give the drink of this cry to your children.
On the occasion of the Hindu festivals
Raise this cry to awaken all.
In the highways and temples, in the market places,
Sing this cry on the bright note E.
From the height of Mount Kailash rises the cry:
'Om Tat Sat! Om Tat Sat! Om!'

Relatives and friends have gathered at a wedding
Forgetting the nature of their Self.
What a pity! They look for joy in this dream-world.
Strike the drum with all your might.
Kill all their doubts and scepticism.
From the height of Mount Kailash rises the cry:
'Om Tat Sat! Om Tat Sat! Om!'

My darling, at the time of thy father's death
Whisper into his ear the message of the Gita:
'Tat Tvam Asi! That thou art! Thou art God, only God!'
Sitting by his side, with reverence
Mingle this cry with thy sighs,
And drop it in the form of tears on his breast.
From the height of Mount Kailash rises the cry:
'Om Tat Sat! Om Tat Sat! Om!'

Revive the dying hearts once more
And proclaim this message as their end is near.
Without hesitation blow this mighty conch.
Kill all their doubts and scepticism.
From the height of Mount Kailash rises the cry:
'Om Tat Sat! Om Tat Sat! Om!'

When the army marches into battle
It faces death outright.
March like Arjuna with a courageous heart,
And from the band may this cry sound forth—
The cry rising from the height of Mount Kailash:
'Om Tat Sat! Om Tat Sat! Om!'

If ignorance ever threatens thee, do not abandon compassion.
Remember, O darling, thou art the abuser, the insult and the
    censured.
Thou art the enemy, and thou art the friend.
Communicate this lesson through thy loving glances.
Reach forth thy hands to grasp the hands of thy enemy.
From the height of Mount Kailash rises the cry:
'Om Tat Sat! Om Tat Sat! Om!'

Stand firm on the execution-ground.
Make thy home in the hearts of the witnesses.
As fingers are pointed at thee
And everyone calls thee criminal and sinner,
Remove the illusion of the spectators.
Show them thy immortal nature.
Bend thy head low to be beheaded
Kill all their doubts and scepticism
And join once more in the mighty cry—
The cry rising from the height of Mount Kailash:
'Om Tat Sat! Om Tat Sat! Om!'

GLOSSARY

ABHYASA   Practice

ADVAITA   Not two. The Advaita philosophy of non-
               dualism is so-called because it holds that God
               alone exists without a second.

AHAM BRAHMASMI I am God (Brahman).

AHANKARA   The ego.

AJNANA or AVIDYA Ignorance. That which is opposed to Truth.

ATMAN   The real Self of man which underlies the
               phenomenal personality and is identical with
               God (Brahman).

BHAGAVAD GITA The Song of the Lord. A celebrated Sanskrit
               poem in which God, incarnated as Krishna,
               instructs his pupil Prince Arjuna in Yoga.

BRAHMACHARYA   The practice of self-discipline including
               celibacy and the service of a spiritual teacher.

BRAHMAN   God: impersonal, without attributes and
               transcendent.

BRAHMIN   Member of the priestly class of Hindus.

BRAJ   Country district near Mathura where Krishna
               lived as a child.

BUDDHA — The founder of Buddhism, an incarnation of God who taught in the 6th century B.C.

BUDDHI — The faculty of intellect and intuition.

CHITTA — The faculty of memory and imagination.

DARSHANA — Sight. A word used as a synonym for a system of philosophy.

DHARANA — Mental concentration.

DHARMA — Righteousness. The basis of the rule of law in the world and of the individual's moral code.

DHYANA — Contemplation.

GIRIJA — A name of the God Shiva's wife meaning 'mountain-born'.

GITA — A song. See also BHAGAVAD GITA.

GUNA — Wave-like principle or mode which pervades the whole of creation. There are three gunas, namely sattva (harmony), rajas (activity), and tamas (inertia).

GURU — Spiritual teacher.

HARI — A name of God especially applied to His incarnation as Krishna.

HINAYANA — The Southern school of Buddhism.

HATHA YOGA — The Yoga concerned with physical exercises.

ISHVARA — The personal aspect of God. The Creator of the Universe.

JAGAT	Ever-moving. The world of experience.
JIVA	The individual soul of man.
JIVANMUKTA	A liberated soul. One who has realised his identity with the real Self (Atman).
JIVANMUKTI	Liberation of the individual soul from the imprisoning force of nescience (avidya) while living in the body.
KARMA (adjective KARMIC)	Action. In particular, a man's past actions which condition his present circumstances.
KOBO DAISHI	A Japanese Buddhist Yogi of the 8th/9th century A.D.
KRISHNA	An incarnation of God who gave the teachings on Yoga recorded in the Bhagavad Gita.
MAHATMA	'Great Soul'. A sage.
MANAS	The lower functions of the mind.
MANTRA	Traditional formula which, when correctly repeated, is a powerful instrument for purifying, strengthening and enlightening the mind.
MANTRAYANA	The Sect of Mantra taken to Japan by Kobo Daishi.
MAYA	The deluding power (shakti) of God by which the universe has come into existence and appears to be real.
MOKSHA	Release of the soul from the cycle of birth and death. Spiritual illumination.

MULABANDHA	A practice of nerve and muscle-control.
OM	Sacred word belonging to no known language and used in many religions as the highest appellation of God.
OM TAT SAT	Mystic saying indicating that God who transcends the world is the only reality.
PANDIT	Title denoting learning, something like the English 'Dr.'
PATANJALI	The author of the classic Sutras on the methods of Yoga.
PRANAYAMA	Control of vital forces through breath control.
PRATYAHARA	Withdrawal of the mind from objects preliminary to the higher meditation.
RAJAS	See GUNA.
RAMA (RAMACHANDRA)	An incarnation of God whose history is recorded in the epic poem Ramayana.
RAMA TIRTHA	A celebrated Yogi and mathematician (1873—1906).
RISHI	Spiritually perfect man.
SAKSHI	The 'witness' consciousness.
SAMADHI	Supra-mental spiritual experience.
SAMATVA	Equanimity.
SANSARA	This changing world.

SANSKARA — Impression left on the roots of the mind by every active or passive experience.

SANSKRIT — Old language in which most of the classics on Yoga are written.

SATTVA — See GUNA.

SAVITRI — God symbolized as the sun.

SHAKTI — Power.

SHANKARACHARYA — A great writer and teacher who is the outstanding figure in the school of Advaita Vedanta.

SHIVA — Bliss. Also a God in the Hindu Trinity.

SHRI — Revered.

SHRI DADA — A great Yogi who chose to teach among the poor of Northern India (1854—1910).

SHRUTI — Scripture.

SUTRA — Aphorism by means of which the teaching, in a highly condensed form, can be committed to memory.

SWAMI — Renunciate.

TAMAS — See GUNA.

TAPAS — Practice of self-control and self-abnegation.

TAT TVAM ASI — That Thou Art. One of the great mystic utterances implying the identity of God and the individual soul.

UPANISHADS	Mystical treatises in prose and verse.
VAIRAGYA	Desirelessness. Non-attachment to objects.
VAISHYA	Merchant caste among Hindus.
VASANA	Latent tendency in the mind caused by the impressions of past experiences.
VEDA	Divine knowledge. The four VEDAS (Rig, Yajur, Sama and Atharva) are collections of religious hymns and rituals which are the oldest known books in the world.
VEDANTA	System of philosophy based on the Upanishads.
VICHARA	Philosophical enquiry.
VIRAT	The physical universe as a manifestation of God.
YOGA	Union. The science of union of the individual soul with God.
YOGI	One who practises Yoga.